P9-CBA-497

Paradise Found

The people, restaurants and recipes of St. Barthélemy

Paradise Found

The people, restaurants and recipes of St. Barthélemy

Robert and Kara Brooks

Buckley Lane Press
Connecticut

Published by Buckley Lane Press, Connecticut.
www.buckleylanepress.com

Printed in Canada.

Library of Congress Cataloging-in-Publication Data is available.

ISBN 0-9743127-0-3

First Edition

Acknowledgements

It is said that it takes a whole village to raise a child. The same is true for writing and publishing a book. In our case, that village exists on St. Barths and includes all of the wonderful people who own and work in the restaurants which are described in this book. They have been extraordinarily supportive of this project and generous with their time and talents. Their faith in us has inspired us to produce the best book we possibly can. Our greatest reward has been being welcomed as members of their community. Our greatest hope is that this book proves itself worthy of their friendship and trust.

Special recognition is due to certain people on St. Barths whose assistance went far beyond the call of duty. These include: Helene Guilbaud at François Plantation, Randy and Maya Gurley at Maya's Restaurant, and the inimitable Andy Hall of The Hideaway, all of whom were enthusiastic about this project from the start and helped open doors which we could never have opened on our own. We also want to thank Nadine Labau at Le Lafayette Club who was the first person we interviewed. Mentioning that Le Lafayette Club was in the book gave us significantly more credibility than we would have ever had on our own. Moreover, Nadine is such a delightful human being that we knew from the start that we were on to something special. Lastly, and most importantly, we want to thank our many friends on our website, www.sbhonline.com, and, in particular, Steve and Libby Troyer of Evansville, Indiana and St. Barths, who share and help nurture our love of the island and its almost mystical ability to elevate the lives of everyone who visits it.

Ilet Chevreau
ou Bonhomme
Ilet Frégate
Ilet Toc Vers
Petite Anse
Pointe à Étages
la Tortue ou l'Ecalle
Pointe Lorient
Anse des Flamands

INTRODUCTION

As everyone who has fallen in love knows, there are few experiences which match the intensity of the early days of a love affair. The world is suddenly very much alive. Music takes on special meaning. Sunrises and sunsets become transcendent experiences. And the most common everyday activities like going for a walk, watching a movie or sharing a meal are infused with new energy and happiness. Life seems very simple and its possibilities limitless.

Even more fortunate are those who learn that love evolves from the giddiness and exhilaration of its early moments and deepens as it is confronted and challenged by the responsibilities and complications of life, and that enduring love not only provides a sanctuary in difficult times but a source of inspiration to create lives of distinction.

Our relationship with the island of St. Barthélemy – or, as the locals call it, St. Barths – in the French West Indies has paralleled and indeed nurtured our relationship with one another. It began with an overwhelming attraction to physical things: to the clear and luminous waters at the end of the very short runway greeting all persons arriving by air from St. Maarten; to the towering volcanic peaks of which the island is comprised, challenging the courage and driving skills of first-time visitors but rewarding them with breathtaking vistas at every hairpin turn; to the secluded and seductive beaches which ring the island; to the remarkable quality of the light to which the French have always been partial which is simultaneously brilliant and vivid yet gentle and soft and seems to suspend the entire island in a kind of perpetual dawn; to night skies so dark, and full of stars that the bands of the Milky Way appear within reach; to the arresting beauty of the residents of the island: French, Black and Mestizo alike; and, of course, to the spectacular food ranging from simple Creole fare like accras, conch stew and cod-stuffed christophine to French haute cuisine classics like foie gras, escargots, coq au vin and duck confit for which St. Barths is justly renowned throughout the Caribbean and the world.

Our early infatuation with St. Barths soon evolved into something much deeper and more profound as we got to know the people who were born on the island or have chosen to make it their home. It is said that the world can be divided into two camps: those who live to work and those who work to live. The residents of St. Barths are definitely of the latter variety, but it would be incorrect to conclude that this means that they are not committed to what they do. To the

contrary, creating paradise on a speck of arid rock devoid of any natural resources is no easy task. And yet the people in St. Barths have figured out how to take their work seriously without taking themselves seriously, and they never seem to lose sight of why they chose to live there in the first place and how lucky they are to have succeeded in doing so. To a person, they are determined to live life by rules of their own making. Many have left their homes in France and elsewhere and followed their hearts to St. Barths even when it was contrary to common sense and conventional wisdom to do so. They smile and laugh easily and often. They cherish not only the physical beauty of their surroundings but the cleanliness and safety of their communities and neighborhoods. It is thus fitting and not at all surprising that the gentle and peaceful residents of St. Barths, to a person, tell the visitor who is inquiring about what makes living on the island so special to look no further than the happy faces of the schoolchildren who are blessed with the opportunity to grow up in an environment free of crime and fear.

Nowhere are the special qualities of St. Barths more apparent than in the more than eighty-five restaurants scattered throughout this tiny island and the people who own and work in them. Unlike the United States, which has become overrun by restaurant chains and where even independent restaurants are frequently owned by anonymous investors and limited partnerships, restaurants in St. Barths are largely family affairs or collaborations formed by a couple of friends, and the owners are present and working in the restaurants every day. Within no time at all, the visitor feels a personal connection to particular restaurants and the people who own them as well as to the island in general.

We have visited St. Barths in good times and in bad times in our lives. In the former, St. Barths always brings us closer together; in the latter, it repairs the jagged edges and resets our emotional and spiritual compass for both the long trip home as well as the journey which awaits us upon our return. The feeling is best described by the great Irish poet William Butler Yeats in "The Lake Isle of Innisfree":

> And I shall have some peace there, for peace comes dropping slow,
> Dropping from the veils of the morning to where the cricket sings;
> There midnight's all a glimmer, and noon a purple glow,
> And evening full of the linnet's wings.
>
> I will arise and go now, for always night and day
> I hear lake water lapping with low sounds by the shore;
> While I stand on the roadway, or on the pavements grey,
> I hear it in the deep heart's core.

After many trips to St. Barths, we finally understand the source of this phenomenon: it is, of course, the people who live there, and they are the real focus of this book. To be sure, the book is also filled with wonderful recipes which have been generously shared with us as well as beautiful photographs of the island, its restaurants and food, but the enduring magic and allure of St. Barths lies in its people and their stories which follow. We feel very fortunate to have gotten to know these people and count them among our friends. They center us and ground us in what is important and good. And by living their lives creatively, passionately and joyfully, and sharing those lives with us, they have rekindled our faith born many years ago that life is indeed very simple and its possibilities limitless. We owe them more than they will ever know, and dedicate this book to them with gratitude and affection.

DO BRAZIL & LA MANDALA

DO BRAZIL

Cured Salmon and Avocado Salad

Coconut Ceviche

Shrimp Moqueca

Tiramisu

LA MANDALA

The Mandala for Two:
Tuna Tataki, Salmon Tartare and Fish Tempura

Thai Curry

Pan-Seared Sea Bass with a Tomato Marmalade

Pineapple Carpaccio

SHELL BEACH AND GUSTAVIA
SAINT BARTHÉLEMY, F.W.I.
05 90 29 06 66
05 90 27 96 96

La Mandala derives its name from an art form used for thousands of years by Tibetan Buddhists for centering, healing and growth. Mandala is a Sanskrit word meaning circle or center, and Buddhists believe that it provides a mirror to the unconscious which enables them to achieve wholeness and thereby share the very best within them with others. It is a perfect name for a restaurant which takes the business of sharing its very best with others seriously although it would be wrong to suggest that the atmosphere at La Mandala is akin to a cloister or monastery. Far from it.

Meet Boubou, the charismatic and irrepressible owner of both La Mandala and Do Brazil. Boubou is impossible to miss. He is tall and handsome and sports a wardrobe that can best be described as *sui generis,* including an unforgettable pair of loosely-woven mesh pants. He is almost certain to be found happily mingling with guests and flashing a slightly gap-toothed smile – a feature he coincidentally shares with Yannick Noah, the former French tennis star, who is a co-owner of Do Brazil.

Boubou arrived in St. Barths in the 1980's at the age of eighteen for a one week vacation and never left. In the intervening years, he has brought his unique and creative vision to a number of restaurants on the island including Le Tamarin, Boubou's (a restaurant formerly on Grand Cul-de-Sac), La Mandala and Do Brazil. His contributions to life on the island transcend the world of food, however, and, most recently, include organizing the annual Music Festival each August. Boubou estimates that the Festival, which draws musicians from all over the world and has grown in a few short years from twenty or so performers to well over a hundred in 2003, brings several thousand people to St. Barths. Reflecting the sense of community which is so characteristic of the island, Boubou does not begin the concerts until 10:00 p.m. so as to avoid cutting into the dinner business of the other restaurants.

La Mandala sits high upon the hill above Gustavia and commands a sweeping view of the town as well as the harbor and St. Maarten in the distance. The vistas from the tables along the outer edge of the restaurant – particularly at sunset – are breathtaking. Reflecting Boubou's intensely personal design and decorating tastes, the dining area is a melange of Buddhist art and sculpture, tables and chairs from Bali, and numerous informal lounge areas including a four-poster bed near the bar. There is even a dining platform built

Chef Kiki Barjettas and Boubou

above what was formally a swimming pool in La Mandala's earlier incarnation as a hotel. Rather than fill in the pool and cover it as most people would have done, Boubou had the vision to leave it full of water and exposed creating a little lagoon in the middle of the dining room which is illuminated by underwater lights in the evening.

The food at La Mandala is similarly eclectic. The genius behind the cooking is Kiki Barjettas, whose abilities as a chef are legendary not only on St. Barths, where he is routinely cited as one of the best chefs on the island, but in France as well where he trained under Bernard Loiseau at the highly-regarded La Côte d'Or in Burgundy. He has been awarded the impressive score of sixteen (out of twenty) from the respected GaultMillau French restaurant guide. Kiki's quiet intensity and passion for food are the product of a childhood in France in which he accompanied his father to the market every Sunday and was given the responsibility to select the ingredients for Sunday dinner. Kiki is the perfect counterweight and balance to the more effervescent Boubou, and their relationship forms the strongest and longest-lasting collaboration between a restaurant owner and chef on St. Barths.

The menu at La Mandala combines the best techniques from French and Asian cooking with an emphasis on the flavors of Thailand. In Kiki's hands, a spice like curry becomes a revelation: always distinctive yet never overpowering and balanced with the other ingredients in a dish. Kiki has worked very hard to perfect his unique combination of these various cuisines including trips to New York in the summers to work alongside Jean-Georges Vongerichten of Jean Georges, Vong and 66 fame.

Do Brazil is pure whimsy, a laid back and funky kind of place right on Shell Beach which was conceived by Boubou almost as an afterthought. A few weeks before its scheduled opening, at a time when there was neither a name nor a concept for the new restaurant, Boubou decided that a vacation was in order and chose Brazil because, to quote Boubou, "Brazil is fun." Accompanied by co-owner Yannick Noah, Boubou made a number of friends in Brazil and returned to St. Barths with an entourage which included Brazilian cooks and artists, and Do Brazil was born. The cooks worked with Kiki and his staff, and the fruits of their collaboration can be enjoyed today in dishes like shrimp moqueca and coconut ceviche. The artists included a grandmother and members of her family who were turned loose to decorate the interior of Do Brazil. The colorfully painted tables in the dining room are evidence of their creative talents.

Do Brazil casts a certain spell: sultry, sensual, almost illicit. The waitstaff wear sarongs and are barefoot, and sway almost imperceptibly to the rhythms of Reggae, Zouk, and Salsa drifting through the dining room as they move from table to table. Patrons, also barefoot and wearing sarongs, wander in and out of the restaurant from the beach for lunch or dinner. Some of St. Barths' most vividly colored and distinctively presented drinks are served at Do Brazil. If privacy is desired, there is a tiny lounge at the top of a spiral staircase which improves upon the already extraordinary view of the water from the dining area. Do Brazil recently opened a snack bar directly on the beach serving panini made with bread baked fresh daily by Kiki which is so good that a number of other island restaurants have asked if they can buy the bread for their own use. In keeping with Shell Beach's reputation as a place for families, however, no alcohol is served at the snack bar.

La Mandala and Do Brazil thus represent a highly original and idiosyncratic amalgam of styles, ideas, fashions and tastes which combine to create two of the most memorable restaurants on St. Barths. Absolute authenticity and complete consistency are not the point, and the visitor is encouraged to relax, go with the flow and be open to new ideas – goals which would put a smile on the face of any Tibetan Buddhist.

Cured Salmon and Avocado Salad

FOUR SERVINGS

Marinate the salmon:
Remove any bones from the salmon filet. Combine seasonings (pepper, salt and sugar) and sprinkle the salmon with 1/3 of the seasonings mixture. Sprinkle parchment paper with the dill and the remaining seasonings. Place salmon on dill and seasonings and cover with additional parchment paper. Weight the fish (you can use a large Dutch oven or other heavy pot filled with water as a weight) and refrigerate for 24 hours, flipping the fish after 12 hours.

Prepare the Gravlax sauce:
Combine mustard, sugar and vinegar. Slowly add the oil, whisking until fully emulsified. Add the dill and pepper.

Prepare the lemon vinaigrette:
Combine olive oil and lemon juice and puree in a blender until fully emulsified. Season to taste with salt and pepper.

Assemble the salad:
Unwrap the salmon and brush off the seasoning. Dry the salmon, uncovered, in the refrigerator for 1 hour. Thinly slice the salmon and arrange on a plate with the avocado slices. Toss the spinach leaves with the lemon vinaigrette and arrange on top of salmon. Spoon some of the Gravlax sauce on the salmon.

Although farmed salmon is perfectly acceptable, wild salmon, especially the Copper River salmon from Alaska which is available from mid-May to mid-June each year, produces a much richer and more flavorful dish.

For the Salmon:
1 pound salmon filet
2 tablespoons freshly ground white pepper
1/3 cup sea salt
1/3 cup sugar
8 tablespoons chopped dill

For the Gravlax Sauce:
4 tablespoons sweet mustard
2 tablespoons sugar
2 tablespoons cider vinegar
3/4 cup peanut oil
4 tablespoons chopped dill
1/4 teaspoon freshly ground black pepper

For the Lemon Vinaigrette:
1/2 cup olive oil
1/4 cup lemon juice
Salt and pepper to taste

2 avocados, peeled and sliced
8 ounces fresh spinach

Coconut Ceviche

FOUR SERVINGS

4 ounces fresh tuna, diced
1 cup freshly squeezed lemon juice
1-1/2 cup diced red pepper
1/2 cup diced green pepper
1/2 cup diced tomato
1 small cucumber, peeled, seeded and diced
1/2 cup diced pineapple
1/2 cup diced mango
3/4 cup coconut milk
Salt and pepper to taste.

Ceviche is a technique of "cooking" raw fish by marinating it in citrus juice. Although this dish is named coconut ceviche, it is the tuna rather than coconut that is, in fact, cooked in the lemon juice.

Marinate the tuna in the lemon juice for 15 minutes. Drain the tuna and mix with the red pepper, green pepper, tomato, cucumber, pineapple, mango and coconut milk. Season with salt and pepper and serve in a half coconut.

Shrimp Moqueca

FOUR SERVINGS

The fish stew known as Moqueca is a staple of Bahian cuisine which combines the influences of African, Portuguese and Brazilian culinary traditions. The key ingredient in Bahian food is dende or palm oil which adds a distinct flavor and color to this dish.

2 garlic cloves, minced
1 red pepper, thinly sliced
1 green pepper, thinly sliced
1 yellow pepper, thinly sliced
1/4 cup of palm (dende) oil
3 tomatoes, chopped
2 onions, chopped
4 cups coconut milk
2 tablespoons tomato paste
1/4 cup olive oil
4 mahi mahi, cod, haddock or other white firm-fleshed fish filets, approximately 6 ounces each
8 large shrimp, peeled
2 tablespoons chopped cilantro

Combine the minced garlic and 1/2 cup of the mixed sliced peppers in a food processor or blender. Puree briefly.

Prepare the sauce:
Heat the palm oil over medium heat in a large skillet. Sauté the remaining pepper slices, tomatoes and onions until tender, approximately 5 - 8 minutes. Add the coconut milk, tomato paste and the pureed garlic and pepper mixture. Cook over medium heat until the mixture reduces and thickens.

Prepare the fish:
Heat the olive oil in a large skillet over medium-high heat. Sear the fish filets on both sides. Add the shrimp and the reduced sauce and cook for an additional 10 minutes. Stir in the cilantro and serve over basmati rice.

Tiramisu

FOUR SERVINGS

8 ounces mascarpone
2 eggs, separated
1/3 cup sugar
1 cup very strong brewed coffee or brewed espresso, chilled
2 tablespoons Marie Brizzard, Anisette or Sambuca
2 tablespoons Cointreau
2 tablespoons Amaretto
2 packages Italian ladyfingers

Garnish: cocoa powder and fresh lavender

Beat the mascarpone and egg yolks until smooth. Beat the egg whites to stiff peaks and gradually add the sugar. Fold egg whites into the mascarpone.

Combine coffee or espresso with the liqueurs. Cover the bottom of a small glass pan with a layer of ladyfingers. Brush the ladyfingers with the coffee mixture and spread 1/2 of the mascarpone mixture over the ladyfingers. Repeat with another layer of ladyfingers and finish with the mascarpone mixture.

Refrigerate for at least 5 hours. Slice into individual servings and top with powdered cocoa and fresh lavender sprigs.

To duplicate the colorful presentation of the tiramisu, heat 2 tablespoons sugar with a teaspoon of water over low heat until the sugar has dissolved. Divide the syrup into 2 small dishes and add a few drops of food coloring to each. Just before serving, spoon the colorful syrup around the tiramisu.

The Mandala for Two: Tuna Tataki, Salmon Tartare and Fish Tempura

Tuna Tataki

TWO SERVINGS

Prepare the sauce:
Combine all the sauce ingredients in a blender and puree for 1 minute.

Heat the canola oil in a grill pan over high oil. Season the tuna with the Szechwan pepper and grill for 1 to 2 minutes per side. Slice the tuna on a diagonal.

Transfer the tuna to a serving plate and garnish with tataki sauce. Serve immediately.

For the Tuna:

4 ounce tuna steak, approximately 1 inch thick
2 teaspoons ground Szechwan pepper
2 tablespoons canola oil

For the Tataki Sauce:

2 tablespoons sliced ginger
4 shallots, thinly sliced
1 cup peanut oil
6 tablespoons soy sauce
1 tablespoon Dijon mustard

Salmon Tartare

TWO SERVINGS

Combine all ingredients in a bowl and let marinate, in the refrigerator, for 30 minutes. Garnish with fresh ginger and basil leaves.

10 ounces salmon, diced
2 tablespoons thinly sliced capers
3 shallots, thinly sliced
Juice of 2 lemons
1 tablespoon wasabi paste
3 tablespoons chopped Thai basil
Salt and pepper to taste
1/2 cup olive oil
1 tablespoon Tabasco sauce

Garnish: fresh ginger and Thai basil leaves

Fish Tempura with a Green Mango Salad

TWO SERVINGS

For the Tempura:

10 ounces fish filets (mahi mahi, red snapper, cuttlefish), cut into bite size pieces
1 egg yolk
1 cup flour
1 cup ice water
Peanut oil for frying

For the Tempura Sauce:

3 tablespoons mayonnaise
1 tablespoon Dijon mustard
3 tablespoons freshly chopped cilantro
6 tablespoons fish sauce
1 tablespoon yellow curry paste

For the Green Mango Salad:

2 green mangos, peeled and thinly sliced
1 red chili pepper, finely chopped
1 tablespoon sweet chili sauce
Juice of 1 lime
2 tablespoons fish sauce

Green mangos, which are picked before they ripen, have a crunchy texture and a slightly sour taste. They can be found in Indian markets.

Make the tempura:
Beat the egg yolk and combine with the flour. Add the cold water and whisk quickly.

Heat the peanut oil to 360°F in a large Dutch oven or wok. Dip the fish pieces in the batter and deep fry for approximately 2 minutes, or until the batter just begins to brown.

The key to great tempura is the batter. The trick is to use very cold water and to avoid overmixing the ingredients. A few lumps are fine. A sticky, over worked batter will result in oily tempura. In addition, be sure to cook the fish in small batches. You want the oil to maintain a steady temperature throughout the cooking process.

Prepare the mango salad:
Combine the chili pepper, sweet chili sauce, lime juice and fish sauce. Season the mango with the dressing.

To serve, place the green mango salad in the middle of the plate. Spoon some of the tempura sauce around the mango and top with the fish.

Thai Curry

FOUR SERVINGS

For the Curry:

24 shrimp, peeled and deveined
1 small broccoli head, stems trimmed and crown cut into small florets
1 small cauliflower, crown cut into small florets
2 tablespoons vegetable oil
4 carrots, cut into thin strips
3 baby bok choy, cut into thin strips

For the Sauce:

1/2 cup chopped cilantro, both stems and leaves
1/2 cup chopped lemon balm
1/2 cup chopped fresh basil
1 tablespoon red curry paste
1 tablespoon yellow curry paste
1 tablespoon green curry paste
1 teaspoon yellow curry powder
1 teaspoon turmeric
3 carrots, coarsely chopped
5 shallots, coarsely chopped
1 cup fish sauce
5 lemongrass stalks
1-3/4 cups coconut milk

Kiki perfected this curry recipe while working with Jean-Georges Vongerichten in New York City. For exceptional flavor, use Mae Ploy curry paste which is made in Thailand and a favorite with chefs around the world.

Make the curry sauce:

Mix the first 10 curry sauce ingredients together and puree in a blender. Cook the puree in a medium saucepan over low heat for 10 minutes. Pound the lemongrass, fold in thirds and tie with string. Add the fish sauce, lemongrass bundles and coconut milk and bring mixture to a slow boil. Reduce heat to low and continue simmering.

Prepare the vegetables and shrimp:

Cook broccoli and cauliflower separately in a large pot of salted boiling water until crisp-tender, about 3 minutes per batch. Heat a wok or large skillet over medium-high heat and add 2 tablespoons vegetable oil. Add carrots and sauté for 1 minute. Add bok choy and stir until just wilted, approximately 1 minute. Add shrimp and stir-fry until opaque in center, approximately 2 to 3 minutes. Add broccoli and cauliflower to pan to reheat.

Discard the lemongrass bundles. Serve shrimp and vegetables in a bowl with a generous amount of the curry sauce.

Pan-Seared Sea Bass with a Tomato Marmalade

FOUR SERVINGS

The flavorful tomato mango marmalade can be prepared several hours in advance and reheated just as you are preparing the fish.

Prepare the seasoning:
Combine seasoning ingredients and toast in a small skillet over medium heat for 5 minutes. Grind in a spice mill or with a mortar and pestle.

Prepare the marmalade:
Heat the butter in a large skillet over medium heat. Add the onions and ginger and cook until onions soften, approximately 10 minutes. Add the sugar and 1/2 tablespoon of the seasonings and stir to combine. Add the rice wine vinegar and the garlic and continue cooking until the vinegar evaporates. Add the tomatoes, mangos, lemongrass and clam juice and cook over low heat for 1 hour.

Prepare the sea bass:
Season the fish with the remaining seasonings. Heat the olive oil in a skillet over medium-high heat. Sauté the sea bass until golden on bottom, approximately 5 minutes. Turn fish over and reduce the heat to medium-low and sauté until golden on the other side, approximately 4 to 5 minutes (thicker pieces will take longer to cook).

Divide the marmalade among 4 bowls and serve the sea bass on the top. Garnish with fresh dill sprigs.

4 sea bass filets
2 tablespoons olive oil

For the Seasoning:

2 cardamom pods, shelled
2 whole star anise or 1/2 teaspoon anise seeds
2 cloves
1 tablespoon Szechwan peppercorns
2 tablespoons coriander seeds
1 teaspoon dried hot red pepper flakes

For the Marmalade:

6 tablespoons butter
2 onions, finely diced
2 tablespoons minced ginger
3 tablespoons sugar
4 tablespoons rice wine vinegar
3 garlic cloves, minced
3 mangos, peeled and chopped
3 medium tomatoes, peeled, seeded and chopped
4 stalks lemongrass, lower 2 inches minced
1 quart clam juice

Garnish: fresh dill sprigs

Pineapple Carpaccio

FOUR SERVINGS

1 pineapple, peeled, cored and thinly sliced

For the Spicy Glaze:

1-1/2 cups water
1/2 cup sugar
1 tablespoon finely sliced ginger
1 tablespoon ground Szechwan pepper
Zest of 1 lime
1 tablespoon chopped cilantro

Garnish: lime sorbet

Simmer water with sugar, ginger, pepper, and lime zest in a small saucepan over moderate heat for 15 minutes. Add cilantro and chill.

Place thinly sliced pineapple on a plate. Top with lime sorbet and the spicy glaze.

GALLIANO
1896
Rhum Vanille
BRAZIL
Saint Barthelemy

EDDY'S

Stuffed Christophine

Avocado and Codfish Salad

Chicken with Ginger and Honey

Coconut Custard with Fruit Coulis

GUSTAVIA
SAINT BARTHÉLEMY, F.W.I.
05 90 27 54 17

Clocks throughout the world are set with reference to Greenwich mean time, a system created in the nineteenth century as a navigational aid to the British Navy pursuant to which time zones were established based upon the time maintained at The Royal Observatory in Greenwich, England. As those who live or vacation in the Caribbean know very well, however, it is possible to set clocks according to a completely different standard which is known as "Island Time," and The Royal Observatory for Island Time on St. Barths is Eddy's restaurant in Gustavia.

Eddy's is on the short list of favorite restaurants for many longtime visitors to St. Barths. They are drawn to the restaurant for the usual reasons: good food, attractive setting and excellent service. But there is something much more compelling that brings the faithful back to the restaurant year after year, and that something is its owner, Eddy Stackelborough, a slight and soft-spoken man with long black hair swept back into a ponytail, a somewhat scraggly goatee, luminous smile and dark, flashing eyes. There is an almost preternatural serenity and calm about Eddy, the aura of someone who is truly at peace with himself and his world. His many repeat customers flock to his restaurant like pilgrims, seeking nourishment which is as much psychic as physical, confident that they will achieve balance in their own lives simply by being in his presence, as if by osmosis. Eddy is also not at all shy about sharing his philosophy about life with others and wanders around the restaurant each evening in his trademark white tee shirt, shorts and sandals, dispensing pearls of wisdom to rapt and delighted friends and guests. One evening, while waiting at the small bar for his table to be cleared and set, a visitor from New York was happily engaged in conversation with Eddy when two young French women walked up and ordered drinks. Eddy and the women exchanged the customary French greetings, but the man, like many Americans who are either unaware of the importance the French place on such courtesies or too shy to extend them to strangers, fell silent and stared awkwardly into his drink. Eddy gently chided his American friend for failing to acknowledge the women. "Why don't you say 'Bon Soir' to these ladies?" Eddy asked with a smile. "Do I have to show you how to do everything?" "Yes!" the man replied. "You are my teacher, and I seek your guidance in all things!"

Eddy was born and raised on St. Barths, one of ten children of Marius Stackelborough, a courtly and affable man who is widely regarded as St.

Barths' unofficial ambassador to the world. Marius also owns the popular Le Select Bar which is famous for its cheeseburgers. As their name suggests, the Stackelborough family's presence on St. Barths dates back to the late eighteenth century when the island was owned and governed by Sweden. Because of the extraordinary kindness and generous assistance he provided a number of years ago to a group of Swedish sailors who were forced to lay over in St. Barths for months while their ship was being repaired, Marius was invited to Sweden as a guest of the King where he received the honorary title of Consul. In November of 1999, Le Select celebrated its fiftieth anniversary with a huge party attended by locals and long-time visitors alike including Jimmy Buffet, a friend of the Stackelboroughs and devotee of Le Select, who entertained the crowd with a number of his songs including, appropriately enough, "Cheeseburgers in Paradise." A similarly festive celebration occurred in honor of Marius' eightieth birthday in June of 2003.

Eddy and Marius Stackelborough

PHOTO: J. ANSBERG

The creator of the famous cheeseburgers at Le Select was, in fact, Eddy. The year was 1978. Eddy had just finished his schooling in Guadeloupe and suggested to his father that they open a small food stand in the courtyard of Le Select during Regatta Week in St. Barths to serve cheeseburgers in addition to drinks to the crews on the various sailboats moored in Gustavia. Marius didn't object but thought it was a crazy idea. Undeterred, Eddy opened his stand and promptly netted $15,000 for a week's work. (Eddy says that the secret to the cheeseburgers is the toasted buns which keeps them light and prevents them from forming a lump in your stomach). But then Eddy did something which is the real key to understanding what makes him tick: he shut down the cheeseburger stand and took the rest of the year off until Regatta Week the following year. Why? Because he didn't need any more money. He knew he could live very happily on St. Barths on $15,000 a year especially in light of the fact that he was friends with virtually every restaurant and bar owner on the island and could usually eat and drink for free.

It was love and not a desire to increase revenues which led Eddy to expand the cheeseburger stand into the year-round business it is today. After meeting a girl named Brigette in the early 1980's and spending a number of weeks whisking her around St. Barths on his motor scooter, Eddy learned that she had been unable to find a job and was planning to return to France. As an inducement for her to remain on St. Barths, Eddy suggested that she take over the cheeseburger stand and make it a year-round operation. Brigette accepted the invitation, and she and Eddy soon married and have worked together in restaurants (first Le Select, then Eddy's Ghetto and now Eddy's) ever since.

Eddy's is located down the block and around the corner from Le Select on the street which runs along the southern edge of the harbor in Gustavia. It is a block which Eddy is particularly fond of because it contains some of the oldest buildings on the island. Eddy remembers a very different and much simpler St. Barths where he and his boyhood friends would entertain themselves fishing on Shell Beach. They were also fascinated by the sharks which gathered beneath a pier in Gustavia where local butchers slaughtered cows across the street from what today are stores like Hermès and Cartier. Eddy's is tucked behind an old stone wall which was built by the Swedes, and the restaurant is sheltered by towering palm and coconut trees which Eddy recalls admiring when he was a boy. Eddy designed the restaurant himself and imported all of the building materials as well as the furnishings from Bali which he and Brigette have visited on numerous occasions. When he built his restaurant, Eddy was informed that he would have to knock down the wall and trees to make room for parking. He refused, citing the history and beauty of the spot, and persuaded the local authorities to allow him to use the street for parking.

As popular as Eddy's has become, Eddy remains as unconcerned about profits and as determined to enjoy life as he was when he first returned to St. Barths from Guadeloupe. His prices are comparatively low making Eddy's one of the best bargains on the island. Eddy does not advertise, reasoning that if after this many years in the restaurant business he has been unable to build a reputation sufficient to attract a steady flow of customers, he should probably find something else to do. He describes having to gently deprogram chefs newly arrived from the competitive French culinary scene who are preoccupied with issues like how Eddy's ranks compared to other restaurants on the island and to focus them instead on contributing to the maintenance of an enjoyable environment for staff and customers

The chefs at Eddy's

alike. Notably absent from Eddy's kitchen are the sounds of shouting and crashing pans which are the norm in most restaurants. Instead, the cooks are very relaxed as they go about their business, joking frequently with one another and stopping to greet friends who appear at various times in the evening, mirroring the character of Eddy himself.

This is not to suggest that the quality of the food is of secondary importance at Eddy's. To the contrary, it is very good indeed. Eddy has simply figured out a way to accomplish this feat without compromising the quality of his life and while enhancing the lives of everyone he comes into contact with. Eddy's secret likely lies in the clock which he uses to tell time.

To quote another famous Island Timekeeper, Bob Marley:

> Rise up this morning,
> smiled with the rising sun,
> three little birds pitch by my doorstep,
> singing sweet songs of melodies pure and true,
> saying this is my message to you:
>
> Don't worry,
> about a thing,
> cause every little thing is gonna be alright.
>
> Don't worry,
> about a thing,
> every little thing is gonna be alright.

Eddy's

Stuffed Christophine

FOUR SERVINGS

4 christophine squash
3 tablespoons butter
1 small onion, diced
4 scallions, white parts only, chopped
6 garlic cloves, minced
2 tablespoons fresh thyme leaves
8 ounces dried codfish, rehydrated (see sidebar) and chopped
1/3cup milk
1/3 cup fresh breadcrumbs

The christophine squash is a pear-shaped summer squash that is often boiled or baked and stuffed. It is known in the United States as the chayote squash or the vegetable pear.

Dried codfish adds a unique flavor to Creole dishes. In order to use it, however, it has to be rehydrated. To rehydrate, submerge codfish in cold water in a large pot and bring to a boil for five minutes. Drain the codfish and repeat process a second time.

Bring a large pot of water to a boil. Slice the unpeeled christophines in half and boil for 20 minutes or until tender when pierced with a fork. Drain and set aside to cool. When they are cool, remove pulp from the squash, reserving the skins. Puree pulp in a food processor or mixer until smooth.

Melt butter over medium heat in sauté pan. Add onions, scallions, garlic, and thyme and cook until onions begin to turn golden. Add pureed squash, codfish, and milk and cook for 15 minutes over low heat until most of the liquid has cooked off.

Fill reserved squash skins with cooked squash mixture and top with breadcrumbs. Place under a broiler until tops have browned and serve immediately.

Avocado and Codfish Salad

FOUR SERVINGS

This dish is called *Feroce d'Avocat* at Eddy's which literally means "ferocious avocado". It earns its name from the generous helping of chili peppers in the recipe. You can season it according to taste and make it as ferocious or tame as you desire.

2 ripe avocados
1/3 cup manioc flour
8 ounces dried codfish, rehydrated (see sidebar previous page)
2 scallions, white parts chopped
1 small onion, diced
2 tablespoons chili pepper, finely diced

Slice avocado and smash with a fork. Gradually mix in manioc flour.

Add blanched codfish, scallions, onions and chili pepper to the avocado mixture. Divide evenly into four servings and serve with mixed greens.

Chicken with Ginger and Honey

FOUR SERVINGS

For the Chicken:

8 chicken thighs
2 cups chicken stock
2 tablespoons oil
2 tablespoons butter
2 cloves garlic, minced
1 onion, chopped
4 scallions, white parts chopped
4 tablespoons honey
1 tablespoon ginger, sliced
1 tablespoon flour
1 tablespoon fresh lime juice
2 tablespoon chives, chopped

For the Vegetable Ratatouille:

2 tablespoons extra-virgin olive oil
1 small eggplant, unpeeled and cut into 1-inch cubes
1 onion, chopped
3 cloves garlic, minced
1 red pepper, cut into 1-inch pieces
1 zucchini, cut into 1-inch pieces
3 tomatoes, coarsely chopped
1/4 cup fresh basil, minced
1 teaspoon fresh thyme

Prepare the chicken:

Rinse chicken and pat dry. Season with salt and pepper. Bring chicken stock to a boil, reduce heat and keep at a low simmer. Heat oil and butter in a large Dutch oven over moderately high heat. Add chicken and sauté until brown, about 6 minutes per side.

Reduce heat to medium and add garlic, onion and scallions to skillet and cook until onions begin to soften and brown. Mix in honey and ginger and stir to coat chicken. Add 1 tablespoon flour and cook for 1 minute. Add enough hot stock to cover chicken and reduce heat to medium-low and simmer for 30 minutes, turning chicken occasionally. Remove chicken from pan and set aside. Increase heat and boil until sauce thickens, stirring occasionally. Return chicken to pan, add lime juice and simmer until heated through, about 2 minutes.

Prepare the ratatouille:

Heat 1 tablespoon of olive oil in a Dutch oven over medium heat. Sauté the eggplant until golden. Remove eggplant and set aside. Add remaining olive oil and onions to pan and sauté until golden, about 10 minutes. Add the garlic, red pepper and zucchini and sauté 5 minutes. Add the tomatoes and eggplant and reduce heat to medium-low. Cook for an additional 30 – 40 minutes until everything is soft. Stir in basil and thyme and season to taste with salt and pepper.

Transfer chicken to plates; top with sauce and chives and serve with ratatouille and basmati rice.

Coconut Custard with Fruit Coulis

FOUR SERVINGS

For the Custard:

1-1/4 cups fromage blanc or full fat yogurt
1/2 cup sugar
1 packet (1 tablespoon) unflavored gelatin
1 can (12 ounces) coconut milk
2 cups whipped cream

For the Raspberry Coulis:

2-1/2 cups fresh raspberries
1/4 cup sugar
1 teaspoon fresh lemon juice

For the Pineapple Coulis:

1 fresh pineapple, peeled and cored
2 tablespoons sugar
1 tablespoon lemon juice

6 ramekins or ceramic molds

This sweet *blanc manger* has its roots in medieval France and traditionally includes almond milk. Coconut milk is substituted in this version giving the dish a French West Indian flair.

Prepare the coconut custard:

Combine the fromage blanc (or yogurt) and the sugar. Sprinkle the gelatin in 1/4 cup cold water and let it dissolve for 3 to 4 minutes. Heat 1/4 cup of coconut milk over low heat. Add the heated coconut milk to the gelatin and stir to completely dissolve the gelatin. Chill. Add remaining coconut milk, sugar and fromage blanc. Mix in whipped cream. Fill ramekins and chill until firm, at least 8 hours. Dip molds in hot water for 2 to 3 seconds and invert on a plate. Serve with a fruit coulis.

Make the fruit coulis:

Puree raspberry coulis ingredients in a food processor or blender. Pour mixture through a fine sieve into a bowl and chill. Repeat with the pineapple coulis ingredients.

MAKING YOUR OWN FROMAGE BLANC:

For those ambitious enough to make your own fromage blanc, you'll need a gallon of whole milk and ½ teaspoon fromage blanc direct set starter (which can be obtained from a cheesemaking supply company).

Heat the milk in a large pot to 170°F for 20 – 30 minutes. While the milk is heating, prepare an ice bath by filling a sink or container large enough to hold the pot with ice and water. Remove the pot and immediately cool it in the ice bath. Allow the milk to cool to 70°F. Remove the pot from the sink and slowly stir in the fromage starter culture. Cover the pot and allow it to sit for at least 12 – 15 hours at room temperature. The mixture will form cheese curds.

Line a colander with a large piece of cheesecloth and spoon the cheese curds into the colander. Cover the curds with the cheese cloth and allow them to drain for 8 hours. Transfer to an airtight container and chill for 2 hours prior to serving. The cheese should have the consistency of cream cheese.

EDEN ROCK

THE SAND BAR

Tuna Sashimi with Avocado Sorbet

Seared Scallops with Warm Potatoes

Fresh Berries and Basil Sorbet

THE TAPAS BAR

Calamari Salad

Pan-Seared Goat Cheese with Piquillo Peppers

Tuiles with Passion Fruit Sorbet

THE ROCK

Langoustine and Shiitake Lasagne

Sea Bass with a Soy Glaze

Braised Duck with Turnips

Roasted Pineapple with Coconut Nougat

ST. JEAN BAIE
SAINT BARTHÉLEMY, F.W.I.
05 90 29 79 99

At first glance, the people of St. Barths appear to be a paradox. On the one hand, they are among the most hardworking, resilient and independent people in the world. On the other hand, they are relaxed, fun-loving and unfailingly friendly and hospitable. Upon closer inspection, however, the paradoxes do not exist. Indeed it is the special genius of this tiny island that by some fortuitous alchemy and combination of light, air, rock, water and the people who call the island their home, those aspects of life which seem contradictory and incompatible elsewhere exist in perfect balance on St. Barths. And nowhere is this phenomenon more evident than at The Eden Rock Hotel and its three restaurants: The Rock, The Tapas Bar and The Sand Bar.

This storied hotel was built on an outcropping of rock in the Baie de St. Jean in 1953 by Rémy de Haenen, the Dutch pilot who eight years earlier was the first person to land a plane on St. Barths and, more than anyone else, is credited with bringing tourism to the island. In addition to running the hotel, de Haenen wore a number of other hats including providing the only air transportation between St. Maarten and St. Barths and serving as the first Mayor of the island.

David and Jane Matthews, the present owners of Eden Rock, acquired the hotel in 1995 on something of a whim. They had come to St. Barths for rest and relaxation with no intention of buying one of the island's most famous pieces of real estate. While vacationing, however, they heard that the hotel was for sale, and David, the son of a Welsh coal miner who went on to become a very successful businessman in England, soon found himself swept up in negotiations to acquire the property. As described by Pamela Parker, Jane's sister and the General Manager of Eden Rock, David cannot resist the challenge of closing a business deal, and, as soon as he made his initial offer for Eden Rock, there was no turning back. Moreover, he recognized that the hotel would be

David and Jane Matthews

a wonderful outlet and showcase for the decorating talents of his wife Jane which, as any visitor to the hotel recognizes immediately, are considerable.

The Matthews purchased Eden Rock on September 3, 1995. A few days later, however, the gods who keep watch over St. Barths in order to preserve its preferred status as the closest thing to heaven on earth decided that a test was in order to see if they were suitable stewards for this venerable hotel. Specifically, the gods unleashed Hurricane Luis, one of the most devastating hurricanes in the history of St. Barths, which destroyed many areas on the island including much of Eden Rock. The Matthews passed the test with flying colors (there was in fact a second test in the form of another hurricane a few weeks later) and turned adversity into opportunity by completely refurbishing the hotel while remaining respectful of original paint schemes and some of the innate quirkiness which had endeared it to both residents of the island and visitors for years.

With walkways and a service road that start at beach level at The Sand Bar Restaurant and spiral up past The

Tapas Bar to the hotel lobby, Eden Rock feels a little like Mont St. Michel, the ancient edifice off the coast of Brittany in France, albeit without becoming an island at high tide or the need for ramparts to protect against invaders. With flowering plants and tropical vegetation everywhere, a wide variety of birds, butterflies and what may be St. Barths' biggest collection of geckoes skittering across the property, however, Eden Rock is a more colorful and beautiful fortress by far. A recent renovation of the Rémy de Haenen Suite, which is literally carved out of the stone beneath The Rock restaurant and boasts a private balcony, outdoor shower and breathtaking views of the Baie de St. Jean, makes it the one of the most desirable rooms on the island if not in the entire Caribbean. Small wonder that Eden Rock was invited to become a member of the prestigious Relais & Châteaux association in 2002.

As any traveler knows, great hotels and great restaurants are not always found under the same roof. Were it not for the arrival of Chef Jean Claude DuFour, and his vision of the hotel as a culinary destination combined with the talent and dedication to make it so, Eden Rock might have joined the long list of distinguished hotels serving undistinguished food. David Matthews hired Jean Claude after an interview in which Eden Rock's chef-to-be informed Matthews that the hotel's restaurants were like a sports car sitting in a garage waiting to be driven and announced that he, Jean Claude, wanted to be the person to put the car through its paces. (Although Jean Claude did not know it at the time, it turns out that David Matthews is a racing enthusiast, and the metaphor was therefore particularly effective).

Jean Claude is Central Casting's vision of what a French chef is supposed to look like. Tall, dark and handsome, with a mane of long black hair swept back dramatically, he cuts a very impressive figure as he supervises the preparation of meals for all three restaurants, stooping over a dish to make sure that the presentation is perfect, spooning a sauce here and rearranging a sprig of basil or mint there, and racing back and forth between the kitchen and the various dining rooms to welcome his guests. He studied at the prestigious Ecole Hôtelière in Bordeaux and worked initially at the Chateaux de Margaux. He then teamed up with the famed Troisgros family and spent ten years at Gravelier in Bordeaux working with Yves Gravelier and Anne-Marie Troisgros, the daughter of Pierre Troisgros whose restaurant in Roanne holds three Michelin stars.

Sonia, Thelma and Chef Jean Claude DuFour

The Sand Bar is recognized as one of the premier lunch destinations on St. Barths. Located on the beach at the base of the hotel, it is a simple but ultra chic space where hotel guests meander back and forth between the restaurant and the beach while the other diners enjoy the food and scenery cooled by large awnings and an elaborate system of nozzles emitting a very fine mist of water. Not surprisingly, seafood steals the show at the Sand Bar with an emphasis on freshness, but with subtle nuances derived from sauces made from various combinations of the over twenty base sauces which are one of the cornerstones of Jean Claude's kitchen. The Tapas Bar, which overlooks the beach stretching from The Sand Bar to the airport, is open only for dinner and is a very reasonably priced alternative for an evening out, offering an astonishing array of dishes paired with a nice selection of wines and efficient service. Sitting at the summit of the hotel, appropriately enough, is The Rock, a veritable gastronomic Eden (an unintended but unavoidable pun under the circumstances) where Jean Claude is given free rein to indulge his creative muse wherever it might lead.

In the mid-1990's, Jean Claude left France for Senegal before settling in St. Barths. During the summers, he returns to France to meet with each of his suppliers. In order to keep his seemingly inexhaustible creative juices flowing, he also spends time in the summer working with famous chefs in other parts of the world. In 2002, Eden Rock sent him to cook with Daniel Boulud in New York. Future trips are planned for Tuscany and Thailand.

It would be logical to think that the man who oversees this culinary mecca would be arrogant, aloof and disdainful of interaction with mere mortals, but nothing could be further from the truth. Jean Claude is, in fact, completely approachable with an almost boyish excitement about his work and life on the island in general. His hands are absolutely enormous, and he greets visitors with such heartfelt enthusiasm as to create the sensation that fingers, wrists, elbows and shoulders have been permanently dislocated. He is acutely aware of how fortunate he is to be working in one of the most beautiful places on earth. He plans on acquiring a boat to indulge another one of his passions – scuba diving. And although being responsible for overseeing three restaurants means long hours, it is not uncommon to see Jean Claude on the grounds of the hotel stealing a free moment with his family (his lovely wife Sonia and equally lovely daughter Thelma) or walking with his yellow lab.

The Eden Rock story would not be complete, however, and neither the hotel nor its restaurants would be nearly as successful as they are today, were it not for Pamela Parker, who maintains a gentle but firm hand on the controls of the entire operation and understands that setting high standards and enjoying life are not incompatible and that striving for excellence is its own reward. After living in Paris for a number of years, Pamela arrived at Eden Rock in 1996. She recounts a conversation with her staff in the wake of Hurricane Lenny in November of 1999, which had winds almost as ferocious as Hurricane Luis and was unique in that it reversed the easterly path which hurricanes normally follow in the Caribbean and backed

Pamela Parker

into the island from the west, when a number of employees asked whether she wasn't planning on simply closing the hotel and restaurants for the season and collecting the insurance proceeds. She quickly dashed any hopes of an extended paid holiday by pointing out that they had the opportunity to do something extraordinary at Eden Rock and that it would be a crime not to make the most of that opportunity.

Pamela never tires of the view of the Baie de St. Jean and has made such a ritual of commenting on it to her son as they make their way to school each morning that, one day, when she was preoccupied with other thoughts and neglected to offer her customary paean to the glorious panorama, her son became alarmed and praised it in her stead seeking reassurance that she still thought it was beautiful. She marvels at the quality of life and spirit of community on St. Barths and the talents of the people who live there. Although running a restaurant can be a competitive and cutthroat business in other parts of the world, Pamela notes that it is very much of a collaborative endeavor on St. Barths. Eden Rock has made it a practice, for example, of not offering meal plans to guests of the hotel to encourage them to try different restaurants. There is a tradition among St. Barths restaurants of freely sharing tablecloths, silverware or stemware when the need arises. Jean Claude is held is high esteem by other chefs on the island not only for his culinary talents but also because he is always willing to provide advice or assistance when asked.

Pamela is fond of comparing getting to know the people of St. Barths to gently shaking a sieve full of sand at the water's edge: when the sand has passed through the sieve, there are invariably a number of colorful stones remaining, each surprisingly distinctive and beautiful in its own right. St. Barths is full of such gems, and a number of them are on prominent display at Eden Rock.

RELAIS &
CHATEAUX
is delighted
Please take your free copy of
TimesDigest
The New York Times

Tuna Sashimi with Avocado Sorbet

FOUR SERVINGS

Avocado sorbet is an unusual yet perfect complement to fresh tuna sashimi.

Prepare the sauce:
Heat the sesame oil in a small sauce pan over medium heat. Add the shallots and cook until they soften, approximately 5 minutes. Add the ginger and garlic and continue cooking until the garlic and shallots turn golden, another 5 minutes. Deglaze the pan with the soy sauce and add the wakame, kimchi, and oyster sauce. Cook on low heat until the sauce is slightly reduced, 5 - 7 minutes. Whisk the sauce and pass through a sieve. Chill.

Make the avocado sorbet:
Bring the sugar, corn syrup, and water to a boil. Remove from the heat and stir in the lime zest. Cool completely. Puree the avocado with the horseradish and lime juice and season with salt and pepper. Force the avocado puree through a sieve and combine with the syrup. Pour into a small pan and freeze for at least an hour.

Assemble the tuna:
Slice the tuna on a diagonal into quarter-inch thick slices. Place the tuna on the wakame salad and top with the sauce. Serve with a scoop of the avocado sorbet and garnish with fresh ginger and toasted sesame seeds.

For the Tuna:

8 ounces sushi grade tuna filet
4 ounces wakame salad
2 tablespoons fresh ginger, thinly sliced
2 tablespoons toasted sesame seeds

For the Sauce:

1 tablespoon sesame oil
1/3 cup finely chopped shallots
3 tablespoons minced fresh ginger
2 cloves garlic, minced
2 tablespoons soy sauce
1/2 cup wakame
1 tablespoon kimchi
1 tablespoon oyster sauce

For the Sorbet:

1 cup sugar
1 cup light corn syrup
2 cups water
1 tablespoon lime zest
2 avocados, pitted and peeled
1 tablespoon horseradish
2 tablespoons lime juice
Salt and pepper to taste

Seared Scallops with Warm Potatoes

FOUR SERVINGS

12 sea scallops, sliced in half lengthwise, tough opaque part removed
1 pound small yellow fleshed potatoes
12 cherry tomatoes
4 ounces young, fresh fava beans, removed from pods
1 ounce sweet peas
1 wedge lime
1 wedge orange

For the Vinaigrette :

2 tablespoons vermouth
2 tablespoons balsamic vinegar
2 tablespoons aged red wine vinegar
4 tablespoons olive oil
2 tablespoons walnut oil
4 tablespoons heavy cream
4 tablespoons mixed chopped herbs (such as parsley, chives, and dill)
1 tablespoon finely chopped lime zest

Cover the potatoes with cold water in a large saucepan. Bring water to a boil, reduce heat, and simmer for 15 - 20 minutes until potatoes are tender. When potatoes are cool, peel and slice into 1/4 inch rounds. Combine the warm potatoes, cherry tomatoes, fava beans, sweet peas and mixed herbs and season with the lemon and lime.

Prepare a medium-hot grill.
Thread the scallops on wooden skewers and grill until just cooked through, turning once, 2 - 3 minutes per side.

To keep the wooden skewers from burning, soak them in cold water for at least 20 minutes before using.

In a saucepan over low heat, whisk together the vermouth, balsamic vinegar, and red wine vinegar. Add the olive oil and walnut oil in a stream, whisking until completely blended. Add the cream, chopped herbs and lime zest.

Toss the potatoes and vegetables with some of the vinaigrette. Make a circle with the potatoes and vegetables in the middle of the plate. Arrange 3 skewers of scallops over the potatoes and season with the remaining vinaigrette.

Fresh Berries and Basil Sorbet

FOUR SERVINGS

This light and refreshing combination is the most popular dessert served at the Sand Bar.

1/2 cup fresh raspberries
1/2 cup fresh strawberries, trimmed and sliced in half

For the Syrup:

5 tablespoons water
2 tablespoons sugar
2 ounces fresh lemonade

For the Lavender Crisps:

2 tablespoons light corn syrup
2 sprigs lavender, crushed

For the Basil Sorbet:

15 basil leaves
6 tablespoons water
2 tablespoons sugar
2 teaspoons fresh lemon juice

Make the syrup:
Combine the water, sugar and lemonade in a small saucepan and stir, over medium-low heat, until the sugar is completely dissolved. Refrigerate the syrup for 24 hours.

Prepare the lavender crisps:
Preheat the oven to 325°F. Heat the corn syrup over medium heat for 1 minute. Using a brush, spread the corn syrup on a cookie sheet and sprinkle with the lavender. Bake for 7 minutes and let cool.

Prepare the basil sorbet:
Finely chop half of the basil leaves. Combine the chopped basil with 2 tablespoons of the water and set aside. In a small saucepan over medium-low heat, combine the remaining tablespoon of water with the sugar and cook until the sugar dissolves and forms a syrup, approximately 2 - 3 minutes. Add the syrup and the lemon juice to the chopped basil and water and freeze for 8 hours, stirring the mixture every few hours.

Fill a glass or flute with the sliced berries. Top with the lemon syrup, a small scoop of the basil sorbet, a lavender crisp and fresh basil leaves. Repeat for each serving.

Calamari Salad

TWO SERVINGS

1/2 pound cleaned calamari
1/2 teaspoon salt
1/2 teaspoon ground pepper
2 tablespoons olive oil
1 clove garlic, minced
3 red peppers, roasted
2 tomatoes, diced
2 tablespoons olive tapenade
Mixed salad greens

Cut the calamari bodies in half lengthwise. Score the bodies with a sharp knife being careful not to cut all the way through the calamari. Season with salt, pepper, 1 tablespoon olive oil and minced garlic. Heat the remaining olive oil in a large skillet over very high heat. Add the calamari and sear quickly on all sides, no more than 30 seconds per side (overcooked calamari will be very tough). Remove the calamari from the pan and add the tomatoes and the roasted red peppers and sauté briefly. Remove from the heat.

Slice the calamari into 1-inch strips. Toss the calamari strips, tomatoes and roasted red peppers with the olive tapenade and serve with the mixed salad greens.

Pan-Seared Goat Cheese with Piquillo Peppers

FOUR SERVINGS

8 ounces fresh goat cheese
2 tablespoons olive oil
4 tablespoons chopped shallots
8 basil leaves, chopped
1 ounce pine nuts
1/2 piquillo pepper (or other roasted red pepper), minced
Salt and pepper to taste
4 phyllo sheets, thawed if frozen
2 tablespoons butter, melted
1 cup mesclun greens

Garnish: julienned carrots and radishes

Whip the fresh goat cheese in a food processor. Heat the olive oil in a medium skillet over moderate heat and cook the shallots until tender, approximately 5 minutes. Add the sautéed shallots, basil, pine nuts, roasted pepper to the goat cheese. Season with salt and pepper to taste.

Form the goat cheese mixture into 1 inch rounds. Wrap the goat cheese in the phyllo paper and brush with the melted butter. Sear the goat cheese bundles in a hot, dry pan over moderately high heat until golden on all sides. Serve immediately with the mesclun greens.

For a crisp, flaky crust, brush each individual phyllo sheet with melted butter.

Tuiles with Passion Fruit Sorbet

FOUR SERVINGS

For the Mangos :

1 mango, peeled and diced
1/4 cup honey
1/4 cup mango juice

Prepare the mangos:
Heat the honey in a small saucepan over medium-low heat. Add the mangos and the mango juice and simmer for 15 minutes.

For the Cream :

1 egg yolk
1 tablespoon sugar
1/3 cup corn starch
1/4 cup milk
1/2 vanilla pod
1/4 cup heavy cream

Prepare the cream :
Combine the egg yolk, sugar and corn starch in a small bowl and set aside. Heat the milk and vanilla in a medium saucepan over medium heat and bring the mixture to a slow boil. Add the egg mixture and simmer for 2 minutes. Let cool to room temperature and mix in the heavy cream.

For the Passion Fruit Sorbet :

1/2 cup water
1/4 cup sugar
1/4 cup passion fruit pulp

Prepare the passion fruit sorbet :
Bring the water and sugar to a boil in a small saucepan, stirring until the sugar dissolves. Cool. Combine passion fruit pulp and syrup in an ice cream maker and process according to manufacturer's instructions.

If you do not have an ice cream maker, you can pour the sorbet mixture into a chilled metal pan, cover and freeze for 3 hours. Stir the mixture every 30 minutes to break up the ice crystals.

For the Tuiles:

1/3 cup powdered sugar, sifted if lumpy
1/3 cup red fruit pulp
5 tablespoons butter, melted
1/4 cup flour

Prepare the tuiles:
Mix together the sugar, red fruit pulp, melted butter and flour. Let rest for 1 hour. Spread the mixture in a nonstick dish and cut into 1 x 8 inch lengths. Cook at 350°F for approximately 10 minutes. Let cool for 5 minutes and roll the strip around a tube that is 2 inches in diameter. Cool completely and carefully remove from the tube.

Put the tuile in the center of the plate and fill with the cream. Garnish with mangos and a scoop of passion fruit sorbet.

Langoustine and Shiitake Lasagna

FOUR SERVINGS

16 langoustines

For the Vegetables:

2 large leeks, white and light green parts finely chopped
1/3 pound shiitake mushrooms
2 tablespoons olive oil
2 tablespoons hazelnut oil
2 shallots, minced
2 cloves garlic, in skin
2 teaspoons vermouth
2/3 cup chicken stock
1/4 cup shredded Parmesan cheese

For the Lasagna:

8 ounces fresh pasta sheets
1-1/2 tablespoons hazelnut oil
1 tablespoon butter
1/2 cup fresh peas, shelled
1/2 cup fava beans, shelled (or frozen baby lima beans)
12 pieces thin asparagus, cut into 1 inch pieces
2 tablespoons freshly chopped chives

Langoustines are closed related to the crayfish but, unlike their cousins, are found only in salt water. They are sized somewhere between a shrimp and a lobster.

Prepare the vegetables:
Thoroughly wash the leeks. Remove the stems from the mushrooms and finely chop.

You can substitute king prawns, crayfish or large shrimp for the langoustines.

Heat a large skillet over medium heat. Add the olive oil, hazelnut oil, shallots, garlic, leeks and mushrooms and cook until the vegetables begin to release their juices, about 7 minutes. Add the vermouth and cook for an additional 5 minutes. Add the chicken stock, reduce the heat to medium low, and cook for an additional 20 minutes. Add the Parmesan cheese and stir to combine. Strain the liquid from the vegetables. Set the vegetables aside and reserve the liquid.

Prepare the lasagna ingredients:
Peel the langoustines, wrap in a paper towel and chill in the refrigerator. Cook the pasta in a pot of salted boiling water for 4 minutes. Cut the pasta sheets into 8 squares (2 x 2 inches each).

Heat the hazelnut oil and butter over medium heat in a large skillet. Add the langoustines and poach for 2 to 3 minutes. Add the peas, fava beans and asparagus and cook until langoustines are just cooked through, about 1 minute longer. Add the chives.

Make the sauce:

Heat a small saucepan over medium-high heat and add the reserved leek and mushroom liquid. Cook until reduced by half. Whisk in the butter and hazelnut oil. Season with the lime juice and salt and pepper to taste. Transfer the sauce to a blender and blend for 30 seconds to emulsify.

For the Sauce:

2 tablespoons butter
1 tablespoon hazelnut oil
2 teaspoons lime juice
Salt and pepper to taste

Assemble the lasagna:

Place a pasta square on a plate and add a layer of the leek-mushroom mixture and a layer of fish. Repeat both layers and cover with a layer of pasta. Scatter the peas, fava bean and asparagus around the lasagna and top with the sauce. Serve immediately.

Sea Bass with a Soy Glaze

FOUR SERVINGS

For the Fish:

4 sea bass filets, 6-ounces each
4 tablespoons olive oil
2 cloves garlic, minced
2 teaspoons minced ginger

For the Vegetables:

1 small celery root (also known as celeriac)
6 pieces asparagus, trimmed and peeled
1 tablespoon olive oil
1 tablespoon sesame oil
2 tablespoons finely diced shallots
1 ounce sweet peas, julienned
1-1/2 ounces cherry tomatoes
2 tablespoons chopped fresh cilantro

For the Sauce:

4 tablespoons sugar
1/2 small red onion, chopped
1/3 cup soy sauce
2 cloves garlic, minced
2 tablespoons sliced ginger
1 tablespoon hazelnut oil
2/3 cup chicken stock
2 tablespoons butter
2 tablespoons lime juice

Prepare the vegetables:
Peel the celery root and cut into 1 inch matchsticks. Prepare an ice bath (large bowl of cold water and ice). Bring a large pot of salted water to a boil. Blanch the celery root for 1 minute in the boiling water. Drain the celery root and plunge into the ice bath. Remove the celery root from the ice bath and pat dry. Return the water to a boil. Blanch the asparagus for 2 to 3 minutes. Drain and plunge the asparagus into the ice bath. Remove the asparagus from the ice bath and pat dry.

Heat the olive oil and sesame oil over moderate heat in a medium skillet. Add the celery root, asparagus, shallots, sweet peas and tomatoes and cook until just tender, approximately 3 - 5 minutes. Season with salt, pepper and cilantro.

Prepare the sauce:
Heat a medium sauce pan over medium-low heat. Add the sugar and cook until it caramelizes, stirring constantly. Add the red onion, shallots, and garlic and cook over low heat until the onions become tender, approximately 5 minutes. Add the ginger and hazelnut oil and cook for 1 minute. Add the soy sauce and the chicken stock and continue cooking for 30 minutes. Pass the sauce through a sieve. Return the sauce to the pan and whisk in the butter, 1 tablespoon at a time. Season with lime juice, salt and pepper.

Prepare the fish:
Lightly score the skin of the sea bass filets. Season with salt and pepper. In a large skillet, heat 2 tablespoons of olive oil

with 1 teaspoon of chopped garlic and 1 teaspoon of chopped ginger over moderately high heat. Place the fish, skin side down, in the pan and sauté for 4 minutes. Turn fish and sauté for an additional 2 - 4 minutes until fish is just cooked through. Repeat with additional filets.

Place vegetables on a plate. Top with fish and spoon sauce on fish.

Braised Duck with Turnips

TWO SERVINGS

For the Duck:

1 3-pound duck
2 tablespoons olive oil
1 tablespoon unsalted butter
1/2 pound carrots, peeled and chopped
1/2 pound leeks, chopped, white parts only
4 celery sticks, chopped
1/2 cup chopped shallots
4 cloves of garlic, peeled and sliced
2 sprigs rosemary
1 tablespoon ten-spice powder (see sidebar)
2 cinnamon sticks
1/3 cup honey
1/3 cup aged balsamic vinegar
1/3 cup red wine
1/3 cup veal stock

For the Turnips:

1 pound turnip, peeled and cut into 1/4 inch matchsticks
2 tablespoons olive oil
1 clove garlic, minced
1 cinnamon stick
1/3 cup vermouth

Garnish: sweet peas, julienned

In keeping with the French tradition, Jean-Claude cooks the duck legs and breasts separately. The legs are cooked *a l'étouffée*, a braising technique that infuses the legs with the flavor of the vegetables and spices that share the pan. The breasts are pan-seared to a succulent medium-rare. The combination is delicious.

Prepare the duck:
Separate the duck legs and bone and split the breast. Rinse the duck pieces and dry completely. Prick the skin of the duck being careful not to pierce through to the meat. Refrigerate the breasts.

Braise the duck legs:
Preheat oven to 350°F. Heat 1 tablespoon of olive oil and the butter in a large ovenproof skillet over high heat. Add the duck legs and sauté until the skin is golden, approximately 5 minutes. Reduce the heat to medium-high and add the carrots, leeks, celery, shallots, garlic, rosemary, ten-spice powder and the cinnamon sticks. Cook until the vegetables start to release their juices. Spoon off any grease from the pan and add the honey, vinegar and red wine. Cook until the liquid has almost evaporated and add the veal stock. Cover and place in the oven for 45 minutes. Remove the legs to a plate and cook the braising juices over high heat until reduced by half. Pass through a sieve and reserve.

To create ten-spice powder, toast 2 tablespoons fennel seeds, 10 star anise, 2 tablespoons Szechwan peppercorns, 1 tablespoon coriander seeds, 4 whole cloves, 3/4 teaspoon cumin seeds, and 1 teaspoon black peppercorns for 5 minutes. Add 1/2 teaspoon ground cinnamon, 1/4 teaspoon ground ginger and 1/2 teaspoon turmeric and grind in a spice grinder. Store in a tightly-covered jar.

Braise the turnips:
Heat olive oil in a large skillet over medium-high heat. Add the turnips, garlic, cinnamon stick and vermouth. Cover and braise until turnips are tender, approximately 20 minutes. If the pan gets dry, add a few tablespoons of the sauce from the duck legs.

Prepare the duck breast:
Preheat oven to 350°F. Heat 1 tablespoon of olive oil over medium-high heat. Add the duck breast and sear briefly on both sides. Add the reserved braising juices and cover. Cook at 350°F for 20 minutes. Remove from oven and add the legs to the pan to reheat. Serve the duck with the braised turnips and additional braising liquid. Garnish with the sweet peas.

Roasted Pineapple with Coconut Nougat

FOUR SERVINGS

Roast the pineapple:
Preheat the oven to 350°F. Combine the passion fruit liqueur, the vanilla pod and the curry powder. Place the pineapple slices in an ovenproof baking dish and coat with the passion fruit liqueur mixture. Roast the pineapple for 1 hour, turning the slices on a regular basis. Let the pineapple cool and slice into smaller pieces.

Prepare the coconut cream :
Whip the heavy cream with electric beaters until it holds soft peaks. Heat the coconut milk over low heat. Add the sugar and gelatin and stir until both are completely dissolved. Chill the mixture. Stir the liqueurs and whipped cream into the coconut milk mixture. Chill.

Prepare the coconut nougat :
Cook all ingredients together until they begin to turn a light caramel color. Spread on a cookie sheet and let cool.

Prepare the mango sorbet:
In a small saucepan over medium-low heat, combine the water, corn syrup and sugar and cook until the sugar dissolves and forms a syrup. Add the mango pulp to the syrup and freeze for at least eight hours, stirring the mixture every few hours.

Assemble the dessert:
Place a layer of pineapple on the plate. Top the pineapple with the cream and a layer of the nougat. Repeat and serve with the mango sorbet.

For the Roasted Pineapple :

8 fresh pineapple slices
2 tablespoons passion fruit liqueur (such as Passoã)
1/2 vanilla pod
1/8 teaspoon curry powder

For the Coconut Cream :

3/4 cup heavy cream
1/3 cup coconut milk
2 tablespoons sugar
1 packet of gelatin
1 tablespoon Malibu liqueur
2 tablespoons Bacardi rum

For the Coconut Nougat :

4 tablespoons sugar
3 tablespoons butter
1-1/2 tablespoons light corn syrup
1/2 cup coconut powder or finely shredded coconut

For the Mango Sorbet :

1/2 cup water
2 tablespoons light corn syrup
1/3 cup sugar
7 ounces mango pulp

L'ESPRIT DE SALINE

Octopus Carpaccio

Pumpkin Curry Soup

Sesame Chicken with Plum Sauce

Lemon, Almond and Polenta Cake

GRAND SALINE
SAINT BARTHÉLEMY, F.W.I.
05 90 52 46 10

It is tempting to say that it was predestined that Guillaume Hennequin, Christophe Cretin and Jean-Charles ("JC") Guy would end up owning L'Esprit de Saline some day. Predestination has a Calvinist ring to it, however, which strikes a discordant note in St. Barths in general and at L'Esprit de Saline in particular. Serendipity is better.

Serendipity is defined as "the faculty of making happy discoveries by accident." The term was coined in 1754 by Horace Walpole, an Englishman who was a prolific letter writer, and is derived from a Persian fairy tale called *The Three Princes of Serendip* in which three brothers are exiled by their father from the Kingdom of Serendip so that they might learn the ways of the world. In a letter to Horace Mann explaining his invention of the word, Walpole noted that "As their highnesses traveled, they were always making discoveries, by accident and sagacity, of things they were not in quest of" and gave as an example the brothers' ability to deduce from the fact that the grass on a section of roadway they had just traveled was eaten only on the left side not only that a mule had preceded them down the road but that it was blind in its right eye as well. An even better definition of serendipity can be found in *The Last Voyage of Somebody the Sailor*, by John Barth, in which he wrote "You don't reach Serendip by plotting a course for it. You have to set out in good faith for elsewhere and lose your bearings . . . serendipitously."

The three princes of L'Esprit de Saline similarly set out for elsewhere and then lost their bearings and ended up in St. Barths. Christophe and Guillaume first met while studying hotel and restaurant management at the Institut Vatel in Paris in the late 1980's. Christophe recalls that during this period the two friends were frequently interested in the same girls but that he avoided head-to-head competition with Guillaume in deference to the fact that Guillaume was the bigger and stronger of the two. After graduation, they went their separate ways only to meet up again a few years later while Christophe was working at the Ritz and Guillaume at the Hotel de Crillon.

JC, meanwhile, was busy establishing himself as the head chef of a rapidly expanding restaurant franchise in Paris. He had never met Guillaume or Christophe and enjoyed a social life free of the long shadow cast by Guillaume. After getting married and starting a family, JC began searching for a better place to raise children where he would be free of the pressures of opening a new restaurant every few months. This opportunity for a new life (and to indulge a lifelong passion for surfing) came in the form of an advertisement for a head chef at Maya's. JC applied for and got the job and packed up his family and surfboards and headed to St. Barths.

Guillaume was the next to arrive, lured, like JC, by the promise of good surf and a simpler life. After working briefly for Le Castelet, Guillaume was hired as a bartender at Maya's, and he and JC soon became friends.

A few years later, Christophe went to St. Barths for vacation having fallen completely out of touch with Guillaume. As luck – or serendipity – would have it, he met JC on the plane from St. Maarten to St. Barths who informed him that Maya's was looking for a maitre d' and suggested that he apply. When he arrived for his interview, he was shocked to meet his old friend and social nemesis Guillaume. As luck would also have it, however, Guillaume had by this time fallen in love and settled down giving Christophe a free hand in the St. Barths social world.

Christophe Cretin, Guillaume Hennequin and JC Guy

Christophe did not get the job at Maya's initially, and he spent a couple of years working at other restaurants on the island before Maya relented and hired him. Christophe, Guillaume and JC spent a number of happy years together at Maya's, but their thoughts eventually turned towards having a place to call their own. The opportunity to do so occurred when a tiny restaurant near Saline Beach, which served sandwiches and was only open for lunch, came on the market in 2000. Pooling their own resources as well as those of family and friends, the trio bid adieu to Maya's (they remain indebted to Maya for giving them their start on St. Barths) and took the plunge.

The first order of business was renovating and expanding the old restaurant. They covered the dirt floors with tile and more than doubled the dining area. They also extensively landscaped the grounds creating a cool and verdant space for diners during the day, and, through the use of spotlights on the gardens as well as the huge rock outcropping which abuts the restaurant, a very dramatic setting at night. They furnished the dining room with tables and chairs from India.

Their roles and responsibilities are clearly delineated and correspond to their respective talents: JC presides over the kitchen where the menu changes daily; Christophe is the ever-charming host, "the clown" as he puts it, whose job is to make certain that people smile and have a good time; and Guillaume is the manager who (at least according to Christophe whose perspective is, of course, somewhat biased) uses his commanding personality to keep employees in line and everything running smoothly.

L'Esprit's success has been nothing short of meteoric evolving in the three years of its existence into a restaurant which averages over 150 meals a night during the peak of high season. Its popularity is a direct result of JC's talents in the kitchen – he coaxes rich and distinctive flavors from imaginative combinations of ingredients while eschewing the use of traditional shortcuts like heavy cream – as well the beautiful setting and personable service. Both Christophe and Guillaume mingle freely with guests, stopping to introduce themselves to each newcomer to the restaurant and pulling up a chair to visit with regulars. There is the distinct sense at L'Esprit of being in on the ground floor of something great. Not content to rest on their laurels, Christophe, Guillaume and JC are brimming with energy and ideas about how to improve the dining experience

and are contemplating opening a second restaurant on a beach serving only lunch.

Equally impressive is the fact that success has not changed the three friends. To the contrary, they never forget why they came to St. Barths in the first place, which was to escape the rat race of life in Paris and enjoy themselves. To help maintain their priorities, they close the restaurant for three months each year. In June, they make an annual pilgrimage to New York City where they visit with and seek guidance and inspiration from their friend and mentor, the highly acclaimed chef Jean-Georges Vongerichten. They are addicted to cookbooks and spend hours in bookstores in New York in search of additions to their already impressive library. They enjoy the change of pace in New York enormously, but only briefly. Sounding like someone describing a fish out of water, Christophe notes that his skin begins to dry out after a week or so in the city, and they are all anxious to return to their island life on St. Barths. They close the restaurant during September and October as well not only because they are traditionally the slowest months on St. Barths but also to take advantage of hurricane season and its huge waves for surfing. They are refreshingly open and candid in dealing with others as illustrated by a conversation with guests after dinner one evening in which they pointed out that there were eighteen places to surf on St. Barths including their "secret" spot which, in their next breath, they freely disclosed.

Such is life when one resists the temptation to plot a specific course, loses one's bearings and remains open to making happy discoveries by accident, and it is entirely fitting that such a story should unfold on St. Barths. The eminent historian Samuel Eliot Morison characterized Columbus' discovery of America rather than the Far East as the "greatest serendipity of history," and, as any visitor to St. Barths quickly learns, Columbus was not only the first European to discover St. Barths, but named the island after his brother, Bartolomeo. Coincidentally, there are also two donkeys (cousins of the mule) who often graze on the grass at the side of the road outside the entrance of L'Esprit de Saline. Serendipity indeed!

Octopus Carpaccio

FOUR SERVINGS

The vinaigrette served with the octopus is also wonderful with raw tuna, sea bass or halibut. Make sure, however, that any uncooked fish you use is absolutely fresh. To substitute fish for the octopus, slice the fish as thinly as possible (see sidebar) and serve immediately with the vinaigrette.

a 3-1/2 pound cleaned frozen octopus, thawed

For the Vinaigrette:

4 tablespoons soy sauce
4 tablespoons lime juice
4 tablespoons mirin (Japanese sweet rice wine)
1 tablespoon bonita flakes
1 tablespoon sugar
1 teaspoon grated ginger
1 teaspoon oyster sauce
1/2 teaspoon wasabi paste
1 teaspoon toasted sesame oil
1 small shallot, minced

For the Cucumber Confit:

1/2 seedless cucumber, thinly sliced
1 tablespoon sugar
2 tablespoon rice vinegar
1 tablespoon chopped cilantro

Garnish: black daikon radish, very thinly sliced and wakame salad

Prepare the octopus:
Remove tentacles from octopus and discard head. In a large pot, cover octopus with unsalted water and bring to a boil. Simmer, covered, until tender, approximately 40 minutes to an hour. Rinse under cold running water and drain well. Cut into very thin slices.

Prepare the vinaigrette:
Combine all of the vinaigrette ingredients and let sit for 1 hour. Pass the vinaigrette through a fine sieve.

Prepare the cucumber confit:
Combine the sugar, rice vinegar and cilantro and toss with the cucumber slices.

Serve the fish with the vinaigrette, cucumber confit, daikon radishes and wakame salad.

To achieve the beautiful paper thin slices of fish (known as an *usu zukuri* cut), start with a very sharp, heavy knife and dip it in a mixture of ice water and rice vinegar between slices. Hold the fish firmly in one hand and, slicing at an angle, cut the fish into almost transparent slices.

Pumpkin Curry Soup

FOUR SERVINGS

2 pounds whole pumpkin
3 tablespoons ghee (browned clarified butter)
1/2 teaspoon cumin seeds
1 onion, diced
2 cloves garlic
8 chives
1/2 teaspoon cumin powder
1 cup coconut milk
Salt and pepper to taste

Garnish: fresh cilantro

The addition of coconut milk results in a rich and silky soup. If fresh pumpkin is not available, you can substitute 2 cups canned pumpkin.

Peel the pumpkin and cut into large cubes. Heat the ghee in a large Dutch oven over medium heat. Add the cumin seeds and toast for 10 seconds. Add the onions, garlic and chives and cook for 3 minutes. Add the pumpkin and cook until it just begins to caramelize. Add the salt and enough water to just cover the pumpkin and cook for 20 minutes. Add the coconut milk in the last 3 minutes. Season with the cumin powder, salt and pepper and garnish with fresh cilantro.

Ghee is an Indian version of clarified butter. To prepare, melt unsalted butter over low heat. Skim off the froth and allow the white solids that form on the bottom to brown slightly before discarding. The resulting butter will have a slightly nutty flavor

Sesame Chicken with Plum Sauce

FOUR SERVINGS

Combine the marinade ingredients and marinate the chicken for 4 hours.

Prepare the sauce:
Mix together all of the plum sauce ingredients except the corn starch and bring to a boil. Boil until the sauce has reduced by half. Dilute the cornstarch with 1 tablespoon cool water and add to the sauce pan a few minutes before you are ready to serve the sauce. Reduce heat to medium-low and simmer until the sauce thickens enough to coat the back of a spoon.

Heat peanut oil in a large skillet over medium-high heat. Combine the eggs, water and soy sauce and mix well. Combine breadcrumbs and sesame seeds. Dip the chicken breasts in the egg mixture and then in the breadcrumbs. Shake off any excess. Cook for 4 minutes a side being careful not to burn the sesame seeds.

Slice the chicken breasts, and serve with the plum sauce.

8 small, well-cleaned chicken breasts
2-4 tablespoons peanut oil

For the Marinade:
1/2 teaspoon salt
2 stalks lemongrass, bulbs only, smashed
1 tablespoon sesame oil
2 tablespoons soy sauce

For the Plum Sauce:
1 cup soy sauce
1 cup Mirin
1 cup water
1 tablespoon plum sauce
1 tablespoon sugar
1 teaspoon grated ginger
1/2 teaspoon minced garlic
1 tablespoon cornstarch

For the Breadcrumb Coating:
2 cups breadcrumbs
1 cup white sesame seeds
3 eggs
2 tablespoons water
2 tablespoons soy sauce

Garnish: finely minced chives and thin slices of lime

Lemon, Almond and Polenta Cake

TEN SERVINGS

For the Cake:

1 pound (4 sticks) softened butter
2 cups superfine (caster) sugar
2 cups ground almonds
1 teaspoon vanilla extract
6 eggs
2 teaspoons chopped lemon zest
Juice of 1 lemon
1 cup polenta
1-1/2 teaspoons baking powder
Pinch of salt

For the Sorbet:

1 cup water
1 cup sugar
2 cups fromage blanc or full fat yogurt cheese
2 tablespoons lemon or lime juice

For a more dramatic presentation, the batter can be baked in 10 individual cake molds. Butter and flour the individual pans as you would the larger pan and shorten the cooking time to 20 minutes, or until a tester comes out clean.

Prepare the cake:
Preheat oven to 350°F. Combine the butter and sugar. Add the ground almonds and vanilla and beat in the eggs, one at a time, and then add the lemon zest, lemon juice, polenta, baking powder and salt and stir to combine.

Grease a 12-inch pan with butter and flour and pour the batter into the pan. Cook 5 minutes at 350°F. Reduce heat to 275°F and bake until a tester comes out clean, approximately 35 minutes.

Prepare the sorbet:
Combine the water and sugar and bring to a boil, stirring occasionally until the sugar dissolves. Cook for an additional 5 minutes, without stirring, until the mixture becomes syrupy. Cool. When the syrup is completely cooled, combine it with the fromage blanc (or yogurt) and citrus juice and process the mixture in an ice cream maker. Let soften slightly before serving.

Serve cake with the fromage blanc sorbet.

FRANÇOIS PLANTATION

Scallop and Black Truffle Ceviche

Shrimp with Red Pepper Chutney

Gingerbread-Crusted Foie Gras

Pan-Seared Pineapple

COLOMBIER
SAINT BARTHÉLEMY, F.W.I.
05 90 29 80 22

Americans are justly proud of their pioneering heritage. The early settlers were a breed apart, possessed of almost limitless reservoirs of physical strength and an ironclad determination to carve out a life of freedom and prosperity in an otherwise inhospitable world. And although the modern American can appear to be a pale imitation of his or her ancestors, this period of history has remained an integral part of the American identity and provided inspiration to subsequent generations that success belongs to anyone who is willing to work hard enough to achieve it.

St. Barths has had its pioneers as well, and they bear a remarkable resemblance to their American counterparts. The first wave of settlers included the families whose names still dominate the local telephone directory – Greaux, Berry, Magras – who endured drought, famine, hurricanes, attacks by members of the infamous Caribe tribe and all other manner of hardship in creating a life on the island. In the latter half of the twentieth century, a second wave of settlers arrived and began the transformation of St. Barths from a beautiful but Spartan island into the idyllic retreat it is today. Happily, it is still possible to meet some of these modern-day pioneers and, through them, experience first-hand the kind of individuals who make such miracles possible. Heading up this distinguished group is François Beret, who built and continues to manage the François Plantation hotel and restaurant nestled high in the hills of Colombier.

In 1968, a politically tumultuous year in France, François and Françoise Beret left their home in Versailles just outside Paris and boarded a small cargo ship for St. Maarten. Like many others before them and since, they were drawn to the Caribbean both because of its natural beauty as well as the opportunity to build a new life in a new world. Following a brief return to France for the birth of their daughter, Caroline, and a year working in Guadeloupe, the Berets arrived in St. Barths in 1971 and made it their home.

Having worked in the kitchens of some of the most famous French chefs of the day – Augier, Tungot, Guyard and Delavenne – it was not surprising that François Beret gravitated towards the world of food on St. Barths. What is remarkable, however, is that this world did not exist in St. Barths in the early 1970's. It had to be created out of nothing, and it was: by François Beret and others who followed in his footsteps.

Françoise and François Beret

During the past thirty years on St. Barths, François Beret has compiled a work resume which is nothing short of astonishing. He was responsible for starting a number of restaurants and food-related businesses, including: The Beach Club, which sat between Eden Rock and what was formerly The Pelican (presently Nikki Beach Club); Boulangerie Choisy in Gustavia (as incredible as it may seem, French bread was not sold commercially when the Berets first arrived in St. Barths); Tamara, St. Barths' first gastronomic restaurant, which was located on the site of the Wall House in an old wooden house built by the Swedes, where Monsieur Beret inaugurated the practice now followed by virtually every restaurant on the island of importing fresh ingredients from France each week; La Tavern, which was the predecessor to Le Sapotillier; The Rotisserie, which is presently located in St. Jean; a jazz club, Club de Jazz, in St. Jean; a second boulangerie in Pointe Milou where Petite St. Barth ("Le Ti") presently sits to accommodate the overflow demand from the boulangerie in Gustavia; and even a yogurt business. A typical day for Monsieur Beret began in the pre-dawn hours baking bread and pastries in one or both of his boulangeries, followed by the preparation of take-out lunches and dinners at the Rotisserie and dinner at whatever restaurant he was operating at the time, and concluded in the early morning hours at the Club de Jazz before starting the cycle all over again after only a few hours' sleep. The Rotisserie advertised "Cooked Chicken for the Price of Uncooked Chicken." On Sundays, it became so popular with the after-church crowd seeking a reprieve from the kitchen that long lines formed out the door, and the processing of orders took on the character of an assembly line described by Monsieur Beret as "Poulet, Pate, Moutarde, Boom!" and on to the next order. As if this weren't enough activity to keep an island full of people busy let alone one man, François Beret also managed to squeeze in a landscaping business, creating and maintaining the gardens for the La Banane and Tropical hotels as well as approximately twenty private villas.

In the mid-1980's, the Berets returned to France for three years while their daughter completed her secondary school education. François Beret spent these years working in the construction business and conceiving a plan which would become his chef d'oeuvre and draw upon the breadth of his talents and experience in the restaurant, gardening and construction businesses: the François Plantation hotel and restaurant.

The Berets returned to St. Barths in 1987, and François Beret tackled the new project in his characteristically energetic fashion. He purchased the land on June 4, 1987. A mere six months later, having worked so hard that he lost over forty pounds in the process, Monsieur Beret opened the new hotel and restaurant just in time for the Christmas season.

It is impossible to appreciate the magnitude of this achievement without visiting François Plantation. The hotel consists of twelve individual Caribbean-style cottages which are perched on the side of a very steep hillside in Colombier and enjoy uninterrupted views of the entire length of St. Barths. The foundations for the cottages and the winding road which connects them had to be dug, hammered and blasted out of volcanic rock. No corner was cut and no detail overlooked in the construction of the cottages themselves which were built of the finest materials including imported clay tiles and marble and furnished with traditional mahogany furniture of the highest quality. The landscaping is quite possibly the most beautiful on the island, a lush and colorful sanctuary for birds and visitors alike. The restaurant quickly earned a reputation as a premier dining experience and boasted an unsurpassed wine list. As François Beret explains, St. Barths wasn't ready for a restaurant featuring haute cuisine when he opened Tamara in the early 1970's. By the 1980's, however, attitudes towards food had changed due in no small measure to the efforts of Monsieur Beret, and the concept of a gourmet restaurant was eagerly embraced by those who had recently settled on St. Barths and the ever-increasing numbers of vacationers.

If the story about François Beret were to end here, it would be a very rich and interesting tale indeed, but there is at least another chapter in the life of this

remarkable man. Not content to rest on his laurels, and sensing a change in the tastes of the dining public, Monsieur Beret has reinvented himself one more time. Beginning in the 2003 – 2004 season, the restaurant at François Plantation will change its name as well as its approach and offer a wide selection of wines by the glass paired with a tasting menu of dishes inspired by a variety of international culinary traditions. The restaurant will undergo extensive renovations and will feature a wine bar and clusters of informal seating and dining areas scattered throughout the dining room. While longtime admirers of the old François Plantation are sure to miss its timeless elegance, the new restaurant will carry on the traditions of superb food, excellent wine and impeccable service for which its predecessor was renowned albeit in a lighter and livelier vein.

And so the pioneering spirit is alive and well in St. Barths and in the Horatio Alger stories of people like François Beret. There is, however, a postscript to his story which is as important to understanding him and the island he has called his home for the past thirty years as any list of his many accomplishments. In the United States, hard work and achievement often come at a price. Whether it is in the nature of the ambition to succeed or the effort required to do so, success and happiness are not necessarily synonymous and, at times, can seem even antithetical. François Beret, by contrast, is a kinder, gentler and happier success story. He is a very quiet man, almost shy, who will only discuss his life on St. Barths if you ask. He prefers to blend into the background at François Plantation, tending to some maintenance chore or watering his gardens. There is not an ounce of arrogance about him. Indeed, François Beret is modest and self-effacing to a fault, describing his beautiful gardens, for example, as requiring nothing more than putting plants in the ground, watering them and letting the sun do the rest. He is an utterly contented man for whom the quality of light on St. Barths still holds the same fascination and allure as it did when it drew him to the island over thirty years ago. His life therefore represents one of St. Barths' greatest gifts to the visitor: proof that a life dedicated to hard work and driven by a passion to excel need not come at the expense of a life well lived.

Scallop and Black Truffle Ceviche

FOUR SERVINGS

12 large sea scallops, tough opaque part removed
1 tablespoon olive oil
1 tablespoon hazelnut oil
Juice of 1 lemon
1 black truffle, approximately 1-1/2 ounces
Pinch sea salt
Freshly ground pepper to taste

François Plantation uses fresh winter truffles from Perigord, which are at their peak from early December to late February, in this dish.

Slice each scallop into four thin slices. Combine the olive oil, hazelnut oil and lemon juice. Spoon the lemon juice mixture over scallop slices and refrigerate for 30 minutes.

Using a mandolin or truffle slicer, slice the truffle into thin slices. Alternate the scallops and truffles on a plate and season with sea salt and fresh ground pepper.

Shrimp with Red Pepper Chutney

FOUR SERVINGS

16 shrimp
1 quart fish stock
2 tablespoons olive oil
1 onion, diced
1 red pepper, diced
4 tablespoons honey
1 teaspoon cinnamon
Salt and pepper to taste
Vanilla pod

Peel shrimp, leaving tails intact, and thread them on wooden skewers.

Bring fish stock to a boil and remove from heat. Submerge shrimp in stock for 5 minutes. Remove shrimp and chill.

Heat 1 tablespoon olive oil in a medium skillet over moderate heat, add the onion and cook until softened. Add the red pepper, honey and spices and cook until the mixture obtains the consistency of jam.

Break open the vanilla pod and crush the seeds and combine with the remaining olive oil. Reserve.

Arrange the shrimp on a plate and top with a little of the vanilla olive oil. Serve with the red pepper chutney.

Gingerbread-Crusted Foie Gras

FOUR SERVINGS

1/2 pound fresh duck foie gras
1 cup gingerbread crumbs
1/4 cup sugar
1 mango, peeled and thinly sliced
1 cup Modena balsamic vinegar
Salt and pepper to taste

PURCHASING FOIE GRAS:
Foie gras is usually graded "A" or "B" by the producer. Although grade B foie gras is suitable for a terrine, a grade A liver, which will have fewer blemishes, is recommended when you are preparing sautéed foie gras slices.

This is an unusual combination that makes for one of the most memorable foie gras dishes you will ever experience.

Let the foie gras sit at room temperature for 1 hour.

Preheat oven to 300°F and spread gingerbread crumbs on a cookie sheet. Dry gingerbread crumbs in the oven for 10 minutes. Set aside.

Heat a medium skillet over moderate heat. Add the sugar and stir until sugar melts and forms a caramel, approximately 5 minutes. Add the mango slices and cook for 3 minutes. Remove the mango from the pan.

In a small saucepan, reduce the balsamic vinegar to 3/4 cup over medium-high heat. Set aside.

Slice the foie gras into 1/2 inch slices using a large knife dipped in warm water. Heat a large skillet over medium heat. Roll the edge of each foie gras slice in the gingerbread crumbs. Add four of the foie gras slices to the pan, being careful to leave room between slices, and sauté for 2 minutes. Turn the foie gras and cook for 2 additional minutes. Transfer to a plate lined with paper towels.

Place the mangos in the center of a plate, top with the foie gras slices and serve with the balsamic vinegar sauce.

Pan-Seared Pineapple

FOUR SERVINGS

1 small pineapple
1/2 cup sugar
1 tablespoon cinnamon
1 tablespoon powdered ginger
1 tablespoon Allspice
6 tablespoons butter
1 cup orange juice

Garnish: vanilla ice cream or lime sorbet

Peel the pineapple and score with a sharp knife from top to bottom.

Heat the sugar in a medium saucepan over medium-low heat and cook the until the sugar caramelizes. Add the pineapple and cook on all sides.

Mix the orange juice with the spices then pour the mixture on the pineapple. Continue cooking the pineapple for an additional 20 minutes. Remove the pineapple from the saucepan and increase the heat to medium-high. Cook the juice until it is reduced to 3/4 cup.

Slice the pineapple horizontally into several slices and coat each slice with the juice reduction. Reassemble the pineapple in its natural state and serve with vanilla ice cream or lime sorbet.

LA GLORIETTE

Seafood Salad

Blue Lagoon

Lamb Colombo

Coconut Tart

GRAND CUL-DE-SAC
SAINT BARTHÉLEMY, F.W.I.
05 90 27 75 66

In every profession, there are people who are recognized by their peers as being the best at what they do, as embodying the personal skills and qualities to which others in the profession aspire. Thus there is the doctor's doctor, the lawyer's lawyer, the teacher's teacher and so on. On St. Barths, Albert Balayn, the owner of La Gloriette, is the cook's cook. Mention his name to anyone in the restaurant world on the island, and the first words out of their mouths will be "he is a very good cook."

Describing Albert as a "cook" rather than "chef" seems particularly apt as he is an unassuming man who serves straightforward and down-to-earth food in unpretentious surroundings. As understated as Albert and La Gloriette are, however, the food is wonderful, and the views from the restaurant, perched right on the edge of Grand Cul-de-Sac, are rivaled only by those of his immediate neighbor, Le Lafayette Club.

Albert, who grew up in Provence, has been cooking since he was fourteen years old, working at a succession of restaurants on the Cote d'Azur before moving to St. Barths in 1979 at the age of twenty-five. Initially, he worked in the restaurants at the Baie de Flamands and Sereno Beach hotels. After a brief stint on Guadeloupe, he returned to St. Barths in 1982 and opened his first restaurant, Flamboyant. The menu at Flamboyant was classic Creole fare, and Albert soon developed a devoted clientele which remains with him today. In 1987, he acquired a piece of shorefront land on Grand Cul-de-Sac and built La Gloriette. From 1992 onward, Albert has owned and managed only La Gloriette and has expanded the menu so that it now includes traditional French dishes in addition to Creole as well as some inspired combinations of the two cuisines.

La Gloriette is a very comfortable and comforting place. On any given day, whether at lunch or dinner, the restaurant is filled with couples, groups of friends and families who linger over meals as relaxed as if they were in their own homes. One reason they are reluctant to leave is because they want to savor Albert's post-prandial rums – ginger, passion fruit and the classic vanilla – for which La Gloriette is famous on St. Barths. But the main reason people are drawn to La Gloriette, and remain for hours on end, is the gracious hospitality of Albert and his wife, Stefanie, who oversees the dining room at lunch.

Just how much of Albert's easygoing nature is innate as opposed to acquired is difficult to say, but there can be little

Stefanie and Albert Balayn

doubt that after thirty-five years in the restaurant business, he has seen it all and is confident that he can handle any and all challenges life tosses his way. Like many business owners on St. Barths, Albert has survived a number of natural calamities – particularly hurricanes. The infamous Hurricane Luis, which ravaged the entire island of St. Barths in September of 1995, completely leveled La Gloriette because of its proximity to the water. There is not a trace of self-pity or bitterness in Albert's description of this disaster. Instead, he retells the experience with the shrug of the shoulders and the detached smile of a man who knows that there are some things beyond anyone's control in life, and that there is no point worrying about or dwelling upon them. Rather than wallow in his misfortune, he rebuilt La Gloriette from the ground up in four short months in time to reopen for New Year's Eve.

On a more frequent but less dramatic scale, Albert also has to contend with thunderstorms which appear out of nowhere and come charging across the normally placid Grand Cul-de-Sac, sending Albert, Stefanie and staff scurrying around the dining room, shutting the large hinged windows which are usually propped open to provide diners with refreshing breezes and the best views of the lagoon. The storms are of short duration – within minutes the sun reappears and the sky and the waters of Grand Cul-de-Sac conspire to produce the kinds of colors which haunt the dreams of lovers of the Caribbean throughout the world – but they often knock out the power at La Gloriette for a period of time. No matter. Albert coolly goes about the business of preparing meals with the only concession to the weather being a temporary inability to serve expresso after a meal – an omission more than adequately compensated for by a second glass of rum.

But the most important source of Albert's calm is undoubtedly the fact that he is doing what he loves. Running a restaurant is second nature to Albert. Indeed, he seems so well suited to spending his days cooking for and entertaining the steady stream of customers at La Gloriette, so comfortable in his own skin, that it is difficult to imagine him doing anything else.

In December of 2002, Albert expanded his operation to include Cocoloba Beach, an outdoor bar and grill adjacent to La Gloriette. Cocoloba Beach serves lunch only and has quickly become popular with Albert's local customers, particularly families with young children who play in the sand and wade in the calm waters of Grand Cul-de-Sac while their parents enjoy a Carib and a panini at one of the picnic tables scattered throughout grounds lush with tropical vegetation. Cocoloba Beach is a logical extension of La Gloriette as a place where people go as much to enjoy the experience as the food. Like Albert, they are happy simply being there.

Seafood Salad

FOUR SERVINGS

1/3 pound sea scallops, tough opaque part removed
16 large shrimp, peeled and deveined
1 pound cooked lobster meat

For the Vinaigrette:
1 tablespoon mustard
5 tablespoons red wine vinegar
1/3 cup extra-virgin olive oil
Salt and pepper to taste

For the Salad:
2 cups chopped lettuce
4 tomatoes, sliced
2 kiwis, sliced
2 grapefruit, peeled and sectioned
1 banana, sliced
1/2 cup chopped basil
1/2 cup chopped parsley

In a medium skillet, heat 1 tablespoon of olive oil over medium-high heat and sauté the scallops until opaque, approximately 2 minutes per side. Chill scallops.

Cook the shrimp in boiling, salted water for 5 minutes and plunge into an ice bath and drain.

Whisk together the mustard, vinegar and extra-virgin olive oil. Toss the lettuce with some of the vinaigrette. Top the lettuce with the tomatoes, kiwis, grapefruit, and banana. Add the chilled scallops, shrimp and lobster meat and garnish with the basil and parsley. Serve immediately.

Blue Lagoon

TWO SERVINGS

3 ounces (2 jiggers) vodka
2 ounces (1 large jigger) blue curaçao
1 ounce (2 tablespoons) fresh lemon juice
1 tablespoon sugar
1 cup ice cubes
Soda water

Garnish: orange slices, pineapple slices, Lemon wedges and cherries

Combine the vodka, blue curaçao, lemon juice, sugar and ice cubes in a cocktail shaker. Shake until the outside of the shaker becomes frosty. Pour into 2 glasses and top with the soda water. Garnish glasses with orange slices, pineapple slices, lemon wedges and cherries.

Lemonade can be substituted for the lemon juice and sugar.

Lamb Colombo

FOUR SERVINGS

Preheat the oven to 400°F. Heat the olive oil over medium-high heat in a large ovenproof pan. Add the lamb shanks and sear until brown, turning occasionally, approximately 10 minutes. Remove the lamb from the pan and reduce the heat to medium. Add the onion, eggplant, green pepper, zucchini, chili pepper and chives and cook until tender, approximately 20 minutes. Return the lamb to the pan and add the curry powder, bay leaf, salt, pepper, and enough water to just cover the lamb and roast in the oven, uncovered, until very tender, about 1-1/2 - 2 hours.

Transfer lamb to a plate. Reduce the braising liquid over medium-high heat until it is thick enough to coat the back of a spoon. Return the lamb to the sauce and serve.

4 lamb shanks (or 8 lamb knuckles)
3 tablespoons olive oil
2 onions, diced
1 tablespoon chopped chives
2 cloves garlic, minced
1 chili pepper, minced
1 zucchini, cut into 1-inch pieces
1 eggplant, cut into 1-inch pieces
1 green pepper, cut into 1-inch pieces
1 sprig of thyme
3 tablespoons Indian curry powder
1 bay leaf
Salt and pepper to taste

Coconut Tart

EIGHT SERVINGS

For the Pastry:

1 cup unbleached all purpose flour
8 tablespoons chilled unsalted butter
1 tablespoon sugar
1 egg beaten
1/8 teaspoon salt
6 - 7 tablespoons ice water

For the Filling:

1 cup grated coconut
2 cups milk
3 large eggs, lightly beaten
1 cup sugar
2 tablespoons flour
1/2 teaspoon vanilla extract
1 tablespoon lime juice
1 teaspoon cinnamon

Garnish: vanilla ice cream and vanilla rum to taste

For a delicious variation, arrange some thinly-sliced mangos or papayas on the batter just before baking.

Prepare the pastry:
Place the flour and butter in a food processor bowl and pulse until just blended, about 5 seconds. Add the sugar, eggs and salt and pulse until just blended, about 7 - 10 seconds. Add the water 1 tablespoon at a time and process until the mixture begins to form a ball.

Form the dough into a flattened round and chill, covered, for at least an hour. Roll out crust and form into a 8 inch pie plate.

Make the filling:
Preheat oven to 350°F. Mix together the grated coconut, milk and eggs. Add sugar and flour and whisk until well blended. Mix in vanilla extract, lime juice and cinnamon. Spoon filling into pastry and bake for 30 minutes until golden on top. Chill until completely cooled and serve with vanilla ice cream and vanilla rum.

LE GOMMIER

Stuffed Crab

Fish Ceviche with Herb Salad

Bouillabaisse Creole

Roasted Pineapple with Antilles Spices

GRAND SALINE
SAINT BARTHÉLEMY, F.W.I.
05 90 27 70 57

Maryse Berry

Le Gommier is named after a Caribbean sailboat which is made from the wood of the gommier tree. The gommier tree is prized for its lightness and strength. Boats constructed of it are built along traditional lines and are especially popular for racing. Sailing, of course, is as old as civilization itself in the Caribbean, and virtually every island has annual regattas and races which celebrate this important aspect of their culture. To Maryse Berry, the owner of Le Gommier, the name symbolizes not only an important part of Caribbean life but the natural union of people and the sea.

Le Gommier is easily overlooked on the drive to Saline Beach as it is almost entirely hidden from view thanks to the horticultural artistry of Maryse and her husband Stefan who have converted what would otherwise be a hot and arid location baking in the same sunlight which evaporates the salt ponds for which Saline is named into a green oasis centered around, appropriately enough, a gommier tree. Le Gommier's advertising is also very limited, and the visitor is therefore not likely to see the name of the restaurant in the myriad glossy brochures which are distributed at the airport and in hotels. It would be a big mistake to miss Le Gommier on a trip to St. Barths, however, as it offers truly memorable meals at prices which are the equivalent of appetizers or desserts at some of the tonier restaurants on the island.

When one steps into Le Gommier, it feels as if one has entered not only a private garden but a private home as well. This is not accidental. Stefan is an architect, and he and Maryse designed Le Gommier to feel like a traditional Caribbean "case" – albeit a very elegant one – and they have succeeded admirably. Le Gommier is quite simply one of the most beautifully appointed restaurants on St. Barths. The authentic Caribbean feel is enhanced by the use of chairs made in Honduras, traditional lamps from Martinique, and delicate linen placemats woven locally in Corossol. The restaurant adjoins the house which Maryse and Stefan share with their two daughters. Above all else, however, it is Maryse who lights up Le Gommier and makes it feel like the warm and hospitable place it is.

Maryse is from Martinique and was a lawyer in a former life. She has been cooking for twenty-six years and operated a restaurant called Lady Creole before moving to St. Barths. Stefan was born and raised on St. Barths. Like the Greaux family which owns New Born, the Berrys trace their lineage on St. Barths to the earliest settlers. Maryse and Stefan built Le Gommier in the late 1990's.

Because of her Martinique heritage, the menu Maryse has created for Le Gommier is based heavily on Creole food. Accordingly there are lots of dishes involving fresh local fruits, vegetables and seafood. In the hands of French-trained chef Christophe Vanda, however, who began cooking at the age of fifteen in a four-star hotel in Normandy and worked in a variety of restaurants in Greece, England and the Channel Islands before coming to St. Barths, traditional dishes are tweaked into something quite remarkable. Thus, filet of beef is served with a morel reduction; conch is served raw with lemon or made into sausage; crispy duck breast is served with a mango salsa. Incredibly, Christophe works entirely alone in the very small and tidy kitchen in the back of the restaurant. He is a study in quiet self confidence and organization. And Christophe's presentation and plating of his dishes is every bit as creative as his cooking.

Chef Christophe Vanda

Le Gommier is very popular with the residents of St. Barths who are particularly fond of Maryse. Like Franckie Greaux, Maryse's initial reaction to being included in a restaurant book was a mixture of surprise and skepticism. Before signing on to the project, she organized an impromptu meeting of friends who happened to be eating in the restaurant at that particular moment. After a short and friendly interrogation about the nature and purpose of the book, they all agreed it was a good idea. The conversation then turned to a variety of other topics, and, by the end of the afternoon, new friendships had been established.

It is easy to like the food at this restaurant. More rewarding still is being welcomed into home of someone like Maryse and becoming a member of her extended Le Gommier family.

Stuffed Crab

FOUR SERVINGS

Place cereal bread in a bowl and cover with lobster stock. Refrigerate for 15 minutes.

Place the crab meat in a food processor. With the blade running, add the shallots, garlic, parsley, olive oil and chili pepper. Add the thyme, bread and stock and blend until combined. Season to taste with salt and pepper.

8 ounces cereal bread
2 cups lobster or fish stock
10 ounces crab meat
2 shallots, peeled
2 cloves garlic, peeled
1/2 cup parsley springs
4 tablespoons olive oil
1/2 chili pepper, minced
1 teaspoon fresh thyme leaves
4 tablespoons olive oil
Salt and pepper to taste

Fish Ceviche with Herb Salad

FOUR SERVINGS

This is a slight variation on traditional ceviche in that the fish is briefly seared before it's marinated in the citrus vinaigrette.

Prepare the fish:
Heat oil in a large skillet over medium-high heat. Briefly sear fish on all sides. Mix the lemon juice, soy sauce and mustard together and brush over the fish.

If you are unable to find wahoo for the ceviche, you can substitute halibut. Halibut, however, should only be marinated for 1 hour or else it will start to lose its texture.

Combine the chopped herbs and roll the fish in the herbs to coat. Wrap the fish tightly in plastic wrap to create a cylinder and refrigerate for 8 hours.

Prepare the salad:
Whisk olive oil and balsamic vinegar together to form a vinaigrette. Season to taste with salt and pepper. Combine the oak leaf lettuce, frisée and arugula and toss with half of the vinaigrette.

Mound a cup of the herb salad in the center of each plate. Without removing the plastic wrap, slice the fish into thin circles. Carefully remove the plastic wrap and place 6 slices on each plate. Spoon the remaining vinaigrette over the fish and season to taste with lime juice, sea salt and pepper.

For the Fish:

10 ounce loin of wahoo
2 tablespoons olive oil
2 tablespoons lemon juice
2 tablespoons soy sauce
2 tablespoons Dijon mustard
1 tablespoon chopped fresh parsley
1 tablespoon chopped fresh cilantro
1 tablespoon chopped fresh dill
1 tablespoon chopped fresh chives
1 tablespoon chopped fresh basil
Juice of 1/2 lime

For the Herb Salad:

2 cups oak leaf lettuce
2 cups frisée or curly endive
1/2 cup chopped fresh arugula

For Vinaigrette:

6 tablespoons extra-virgin olive oil
2 tablespoons balsamic vinegar
1 teaspoon fresh lime juice
Sea salt and freshly ground pepper to taste

Bouillabaisse Creole

FOUR SERVINGS

For the Bouillabaisse:

8 ounce tuna steak
4 ounce red snapper filet
4 ounce halibut filet,
12 large shrimp
2 tablespoons olive oil
2 tablespoons chopped shallots
1 onion, chopped
1 red pepper, diced
1 garlic clove, crushed
1 sprig thyme
1 bay leaf
1 cup of fish stock
4 ounces cherry tomatoes, halved
1 teaspoon tomato paste
1 small chili pepper
1/8 teaspoon saffron
Juice of 1/2 lemon
2 tablespoons chopped fresh cilantro

For the Scallion Mashed Potatoes:

1 pound Idaho potatoes
4 tablespoons butter, cut into small pieces
1/4 cup heavy cream
1/4 cup milk
4 scallions, white and light green parts only, chopped

Bouillabaisse, the famous Mediterranean fish stew, was traditionally made with fish that the fisherman could not sell at the end of the day. It is particularly outstanding, however, when prepared with the tuna, red snapper, halibut and shrimp which are called for in this recipe.

Prepare the bouillabaisse:
Cut the tuna, red snapper and halibut into 1-inch pieces. Peel and devein the shrimp. Heat the olive oil in a large skillet over medium heat. Add the shallots, onions, red pepper, garlic, thyme and bay leaf and sauté until the onion softens, approximately 10 minutes.

Increase the heat to medium-high and add the tuna, red snapper and halibut, searing the fish on all sides. Add the shrimp and sauté for 1 minute. Reduce the heat to medium and add the fish stock, cherry tomatoes, tomato paste, saffron and whole chili pepper to the pan and simmer for 5 minutes. Stir in lemon juice.

Prepare the scallion mashed potatoes:
Peel the potatoes and cut into 1-inch pieces. Bring a large pot of salted water to a boil. Boil potatoes for 20 minutes or until tender. While potatoes are cooking, combine milk and cream in a small saucepan and heat until hot. Drain potatoes in a colander and force through a potato ricer into a large bowl. Add butter, milk, cream and scallions and stir gently.

For light and fluffy mashed potatoes, soak the potatoes (peeled and cut into 1-inch pieces) in a bowl of cold water for 10 minutes. This will remove the excess starch. Drain and rinse potatoes before cooking.

Serve immediately or transfer potatoes to a double boiler placed over hot water.

Prepare the fried cucumber:
Heat oil in a medium skillet over medium-high heat. Dredge the cucumber slices in the flour, shaking off the excess, and fry the cucumber slices in the oil for 2 minutes per side. Drain cucumber slices on a plate covered with a paper towel.

Garnish bouillabaisse with cilantro and serve with fried cucumbers and scallion mashed potatoes.

For the Fried Cucumber:

1 tablespoon olive oil
1 cucumber, peeled and sliced
1 tablespoon flour
Salt and pepper to taste

Roasted Pineapple with Antilles Spices

FOUR SERVINGS

1 large pineapple, peeled, cored, and cut into 4 slices
1 cup water
2 cups brown sugar
1 cinnamon stick
1 tablespoon Szechwan pepper
1 star anise
1 vanilla pod, sliced lengthwise

3 cups vanilla ice cream

Preheat oven to 450°F.

In a large saucepan, combine water and 1-1/2 cups brown sugar over medium-high heat. Bring the mixture to a low boil and simmer for 10 minutes. Add the cinnamon stick, pepper, star anise and the vanilla pod and remove from the heat.

Roll the pineapple slices in the remaining brown sugar and roast in a roasting pan in the oven for 15 minutes. Add the syrup to the pineapple and allow it to cook for an additional hour, turning the slices from time to time.

Remove the pineapple from the roasting pan and chill in the refrigerator for at least 30 minutes and up to 2 days.

Slice the pineapple at an angle and top it with the vanilla ice cream. Spoon the syrup around the pineapple and garnish with brown sugar and pineapple leaves.

THE HIDEAWAY

Cod Fritters

California Pizza

Scallops Provençale

The Colonel

SAINT JEAN
SAINT BARTHÉLEMY, F.W.I.
05 90 27 63 62

Andy Hall, the owner of The Hideaway, is an institution on St. Barths not only because of his physical stature (at 6'5" tall he literally towers over everyone else on the island) but because of his infectious bonhomie – a personality trait the French have long considered their own. Indeed, it is somewhat remarkable that on an island that already knows how to enjoy itself, this British expatriate continues to show the French new ways to put the joie into vivre. The float he and his friends create each year for Carnival has become one of the highlights of the parade. His promotional campaign for The Hideaway consists of poking fun at himself and his restaurant, touting the warm beer, lousy food, views of the car park and a staff who have either been fired from worse restaurants or escaped from mental institutions. Despite this fact, or, more precisely, because of it, The Hideaway is packed at lunch and dinner. In October of 2002, Andy decided to throw a party for the entire island to celebrate the fact that the restaurant had been open for five years. Over 3,000 people showed up to commemorate the occasion, and it wasn't just for the free food.

Andy got his start in the working world in the mid-1980's as a clerk in a large insurance company in London. After only a short time on the job, however, he decided that a change was in order and walked into the office of his supervisor, a mid-level manager in the company, and informed him that he was quitting and moving to France to pick grapes for the wine harvest. His boss was incredulous and explained that in twenty years, if Andy continued to work very hard, he, too, could be a supervisor at the company. Thinking "That's precisely my point" but saying something polite instead like "That's very kind but I really must be going," Andy said goodbye to his boss and the world of London insurance and set off for France one fine morning in May to begin his new life in the French wine business.

The Hideaway Team

Grapes, of course, are not harvested in May, a fact which dawned on Andy only after his arrival in France. Short of funds, he took a job in a café on a beach in a town near Bordeaux and began cooking crêpes and hamburgers. While working at the café, he became good friends with its manager, Kiki Laporte, the present owner of the local St. Barths radio station Radio Transat (and a collaborator of Andy's in creating their annual float for the Carnival parade). After making a number of trips to St. Barths, Kiki decided to move there and suggested that Andy join him in relocating to the island. Although he had never visited St. Barths, Andy agreed and made the move in the late 1980's.

One of his first jobs was as a bartender at the legendary Autour de Rocher, an odd menagerie of a restaurant, bar and shops which was the scene of many wild and memorable evenings before it burned down in the early 1990's. Soon after starting work at Autour de Rocher, however, Andy's career as a bartender was almost cut short. A man Andy had never seen before ordered a Heineken and then walked away from the bar without paying. Andy accosted the stranger, shouting "Hey, Mate! That'll be five bucks!" The bar fell silent as the man turned and faced Andy. "Do you know who I am?" the man asked. Andy said no. "I'm Jimmy Buffett, and I own this bar." "Well you better be!" Andy said, grinning sheepishly, and all was forgiven.

After the fire at Autour de Rocher, Andy worked a succession of other bartending jobs including stints at the Bar de l'Oubli and the Jungle Café before deciding to open The Hideaway in 1997. It was not an easy transition for Andy as he attempted to juggle the responsibilities of restaurant ownership while maintaining his old hours and social life as a bartender. After a year or so, he decided he really wanted the restaurant to succeed and became more serious about the day-to-day management of the business. Fortunately, "serious" is a relative term for Andy, and adopting a more business-like approach to The Hideaway did not mean that he abandoned the idea of having fun and making certain that everyone around him does as well.

Of course, the liveliest and most enjoyable restaurant atmosphere in the world would mean little if the food didn't hold its own, and the food at The Hideaway does not disappoint. The most popular item on the menu is the thin crust pizza. The toppings are varied and run the gamut from the traditional California pizza featuring tomatoes, basil and fresh mozzarella to more exotic offerings which have a French-Caribbean flair, including an artichoke heart, pineapple and salmon combination. The salads are excellent as is a fish dish which diners cook on hot stones at their tables. The wine list is without question the most reasonable on the island. The traditional after-dinner digestif, vanilla rum, is made on the premises and is noteworthy because it comes in a seemingly bottomless little carafe which is refilled wordlessly for as long as diners care to sit at their tables.

All in all, The Hideaway is not only a guaranteed good time in St. Barths – sort of like getting invited to a really good party with a great host – but is also a nice and even welcome respite from its pricier competitors serving more elaborate food . When asked the key to his happiness, Andy's reply is simple: he realizes that for most people, even the most successful people in the world, coming to St. Barths for a week or two is one of the highlights of their year, and he never forgets how lucky he is to have abandoned the world of London insurance and to have made the island his home.

Chez ANDY
The Hideaway
114

Cod Fritters

FOUR SERVINGS

10 ounces dried cod
1 onion, finely diced
1 garlic clove, minced
2 small chili peppers, minced
2 tablespoons freshly chopped chives
1-1/3 cups flour
3 eggs
2 packages (4-1/2 teaspoons) active dry yeast
2 tablespoons red wine vinegar
Corn oil for frying

This classic dish, also known as Accra, is served at a number of restaurants on the island and is a favorite at The Hideaway.

Soak the cod for 24 hours, changing the water 2 to 3 times. Chop the cod and puree with the onion, garlic, chili pepper and chives.

Dilute the yeast in the vinegar and let it sit for 5 minutes. Add to the pureed cod mixture. Add the eggs and slowly add in the flour, 1/2 cup at a time until you achieve a thick paste.

Heat the corn oil to 160°F and dip 1 tablespoon of the cod mixture into the oil at a time and fry for 5 minutes, until golden brown.

California Pizza

FOUR SERVINGS

Prepare the dough:
Dissolve the yeast in a cup of lukewarm water. Let sit for 5 minutes. Add the olive oil, salt and remaining water. Put 2 cups of flour in a food processor fitted with a dough blade and add the yeast mixture. Pulse briefly and slowly add the remaining cup of flour. Knead for 10 minutes. Transfer dough to a large bowl and set in a warm place to rise for 1 hour. Punch down and let sit for 10 minutes. Divide into 4 balls.

To peel the tomatoes, make a small cut in the bottom of each tomato and plunge into boiling water for 5 - 10 seconds. The skin will easily peel off.

Prepare the sauce:
Peel and seed the tomatoes. Chop and sauté over medium heat for 20 minutes. Stir in the basil, olive oil and salt. Puree sauce.

Assemble the pizza:
Preheat oven to 450°F. Roll each ball out into a very thin circle. Add 1 cup of sauce to each pizza and spread evenly leaving 1/2 inch on the sides. Sprinkle on the mozzarella cheese, goat cheese, tomato slices, garlic, basil, parsley and oregano. Cook for 8 - 10 minutes and serve immediately.

For the Dough:

1 package (2-1/4 teaspoons) active dry yeast
1-1/4 cups water
2 tablespoons olive oil
Pinch of salt
3 cups flour

For the Sauce:

2 pounds tomatoes
1/2 cup freshly chopped basil
2 teaspoons olive oil
Pinch of salt

For the Toppings:

4 cups freshly grated mozzarella cheese
8 ounces fresh goat cheese
1 tomato, thinly sliced
1 clove garlic, minced
1/2 cup freshly chopped basil
2 tablespoons freshly chopped parsley
1 tablespoon oregano

Andy Hall and the Hideaway's famous pizza

Scallops Provençale

FOUR SERVINGS

36 sea scallops, tough opaque part removed
2 tablespoons olive oil
8 tomatoes, peeled, seeded and diced
1 onion, diced
1 carrot, peeled and chopped
1 red pepper, diced
1/2 cup water
1 tablespoon herbes de Provence
1/2 cup pitted black olives
Salt and pepper to taste

Garnish: fresh dill springs and black olives

Simmer tomatoes, onions, carrots, and red pepper in 1/2 cup water in a medium saucepan over moderate heat for 20 minutes. Add the herbes de Provence, olives, salt, and pepper and simmer for 5 additional minutes. Cool sauce and blend in a food processor or blender until smooth.

Heat oil in a large skillet over medium-high heat. Sear scallops for approximately 1-2 minutes per side.

Remove the scallops and discard any remaining oil. Add the sauce to the pan and reheat.

Serve the scallops, topped with the sauce, on basmati rice and garnish with fresh dill and black olives.

The Colonel

TWO SERVINGS

Leave it to a former bartender to feature a drink masquerading as a dessert which, at the Hideaway, is followed by a bottomless carafe of homemade vanilla rum (see recipe at sidebar).

4 scoops lime sorbet
2 shots high quality vodka, such as Grey Goose

Spoon 2 scoops of sorbet into each glass. Top with a shot of vodka and serve immediately.

MAKING YOUR OWN VANILLA RUM
There are as many different recipes for vanilla rum as there are restaurants serving it on St. Barths. A traditional method calls for 4 cups dark rum, 2 cups light rum, 10 -12 vanilla beans, 2 cups sugar, 2 cups water and 1 tablespoon of glycerin. Combine the rum with the vanilla beans and refrigerate for 1 month. Remove the vanilla beans and add the sugar, water and glycerin. Store for an additional 1 -2 months before serving. For those unwilling or unable to wait three months for their rum, Andy Hall recommends mixing 2 parts sugar cane syrup, 1 part vanilla extract, 5 parts Mount Gay rum and 2 parts Myers's Dark rum. According to Andy you should "Wait 20 seconds if you can, and then start drinking."

YAMAHA
CORAIL DE FEU

LE LAFAYETTE CLUB

Pina Colada

Avocado Creole

Shrimp Provençale

Tarte Tatin

GRAND CUL-DE-SAC
SAINT BARTHÉLEMY, F.W.I.
05 90 27 62 51

It is said that some of the most powerful memories derive from the senses, and, of all of the sensual experiences on St. Barths, none is more vivid and enduring than the vistas of the sea at the island's many inlets and beaches. Whether it is the tranquil turquoise cove at Shell Beach in Gustavia, the contrast of the cerulean blue and ultramarine at the surf breaks off St. Jean and Lorient, or the broad sweep of azure which greets the visitor to Saline and Gouverneur, the waters surrounding St. Barths conjure up the full range of the artist's palette and remain clearly etched in the mind of the visitor long after other memories have begun to fade.

At the far end of St. Barths, in Grand Cul-de-Sac, lies a lagoon where the water is so clear and luminescent as to be ethereal. The view is, in fact, so arresting that it would be possible to spend an entire vacation in St. Barths doing nothing but staring at the water and marveling at its brilliance. Happily, it is also possible to savor wonderful food while indulging in such reveries at Le Lafayette Club, a restaurant built right on the beach by Georges and Nadine Labau over twenty-five years ago.

Nadine discovered St. Barths in 1971 while working as an au pair in New York. The family she worked for had announced that it was going to the island for vacation but that it had no intention of bringing Nadine along. Whether through intuition or not, Nadine decided that she really had to make the trip and pleaded with the family to let her accompany them. They agreed but only after she offered to buy her own plane ticket. It was love at first sight for Nadine. When she returned to New York, she called her boyfriend, Georges, who owned a real estate business in Toulouse, and announced that they had to move to St. Barths. They arrived on the island eight months later and have never left.

To appreciate just how bold a step such a move was for Nadine and Georges and others who left jobs, family and friends behind and moved to St. Barths during this period, it is important to understand that the island was nothing more than a sleepy backwater at the time with few of the hotels, restaurants and modern conveniences which exist today. The first plane arrived in the 1940's when a Dutch pilot, Rémy de Haenen, made a daring landing on a pasture in St. Jean where the airport sits today. For years, the only way for visitors to get to St. Barths by air was to call de Haenen after arriving in St. Maarten and wait for him to finish whatever he was doing and fly over and pick them up. The runway was

eventually paved, but people continued to wait for flights under a tree until a terminal was constructed in the 1980's. In the 1950's, there were only three automobiles on the island. Telephones were introduced to St. Barths in the 1960's, but service was initially limited to fifteen phones.

As undeveloped as St. Barths was at the time, Grand Cul-de-Sac was essentially in its primordial natural state and as far from the limited commercial activity in Gustavia and St. Jean as it was possible to get. Possessing the courage and vision of true pioneers, however, (with no doubt a dash of being young, foolish and in love), and ignoring the howls of protest and dire warnings by their respective families of imminent financial ruin, Nadine and Georges decided to buy the land on which Le Lafayette Club presently sits and build the restaurant.

Nadine's eyes sparkle as she recounts the way she and Georges lived in those simpler times. They ate the fish and lobsters which Georges, an avid diver, would catch with a spear or by hand. They adopted a couple of young goats as pets before releasing them into the wild after learning the hard way how difficult they are to housebreak. They finished construction of the restaurant in 1975 and named it after their favorite café in Toulouse. Despite their proximity to the water, they even built the first swimming pool on the island for guests of the restaurant and constructed it so well that it has survived a number of hurricanes, including the devastating Hurricane Luis in September of 1995.

Initially, Le Lafayette Club was open for lunch and dinner. Because of its extraordinary location, where guests sit in the shade of sea grape, palm and coconut trees and sink their toes into soft sand at tables placed literally on the beach all the while soaking in the breathtaking vista of Grand Cul-de-Sac, Le Lafayette Club quickly became so popular for lunch that the dinner service was discontinued.

In 1982, Nadine opened a small clothing boutique in the back of the restaurant and instituted the fashion show which has become a fixture on St. Barths. Every lunch, a lithe and leggy model passes discreetly and unobtrusively from table to table in various outfits from the boutique. Georges, whom Nadine likes to describe as "a show onto himself," often sits at a table in the back of the restaurant enjoying the company of friends and surveying the lunch scene with a look of utter contentment. Although such an

George, Nadine and Elyse Labau

experience might be a little over-the-top if it were attempted in the United States, it is low-key and relaxed in St. Barths. Nadine's first model was a cousin who was also an architect. Scores of models have come and gone since then, and Nadine remembers them all fondly as members of her extended restaurant family. Le Lafayette Club has also been a home-away-from-home for Nadine's and Georges's immediate family. Their daughter, Elyse, was brought to the restaurant for the first time when she was only five weeks old in a basket and spent many hours over the years doing her homework at one of the tables in the dining area.

Le Lafayette Club's many admirers are insistent that Nadine and Georges do nothing to alter this little slice of paradise in any way. Accordingly, Georges and Nadine go to extraordinary lengths to keep things as they have always been

even to the point of retaining a small box to hold cash and credit card receipts which they used when the restaurant first opened rather than replace it with a cash register. The customer list reads like a Who's Who of the rich and famous (whose identities can be ascertained from the graffiti which is lovingly preserved on the bathroom walls), but, in typical St. Barths' fashion, the presence of assorted luminaries is not a big deal, and ordinary folks receive just as warm a reception and feel just as welcome as the more famous guests. Indeed, perhaps the most remarkable aspect of Le Lafayette Club is that by serving excellent food in an incomparable setting with gracious service augmented by a fashion show, Nadine and Georges have succeeded in creating an enchanted little world where everyone leaves feeling a little bit more glamorous than when they arrived.

Pina Colada

TWO SERVINGS

Le Lafayette Club is famous for its enormous pina coladas, and although the view of Grand Cul-de-Sac is a wonderful additional ingredient, it is not an essential one. Here's how to recreate some of the magic of Le Lafayette Club at home.

Combine the first 4 ingredients in a blender. Blend for 1 minute. Pour into a large glass and top with a dusting of cinnamon and fruit garnishes.

1/4 cup Coco Lopez or sweetened coconut milk
1/4 cup rum
1/2 cup pineapple juice
2 cups ice
1/4 teaspoon ground cinnamon
Fruit garnishes: orange slices, lemon slices, lime slices and cherries

Shrimp Provençale and Le Lafayette Club's Pina Colada

Avocado Creole

FOUR SERVINGS

4 ripe avocados

For the Creole Sauce:

1 small onion, diced
6 scallions, white parts chopped
1 teaspoon fresh thyme
1 clove garlic, minced
1/2 teaspoon chopped chili pepper
1 cup extra-virgin olive oil
2 tablespoons fresh lime juice
1–2 tablespoons water
Salt and pepper to taste

Sauté the onion over medium-low heat until it turns golden. Remove from heat and combine with the scallions, thyme, garlic, chili pepper, olive oil and lime juice. Add water as needed to balance the acidity of the lime juice. Season with salt and pepper. The Creole sauce can be made 2 hours in advance.

Peel the avocado and slice it in half lengthwise and slice each half into 6 to 7 long pieces. Fan the slices from half of an avocado on a plate and top with the Creole sauce.

Avocados are one of the few fruits that do not begin to ripen until they are picked. As such, it is a good idea to purchase slightly unripe avocados, which are less likely to be bruised, and let them ripen on the counter for a few days before using them.

Shrimp Provençale

FOUR SERVINGS

For the Shrimp:

1 pound shrimp
1 tablespoon olive oil
2 shallots, finely chopped
1 clove garlic, minced
1 pound tomatoes, peeled, seeded and chopped
1/4 cup parsley, chopped
Salt and pepper

For the Curried Rice:

1 large onion, diced
1 tablespoon olive oil
2 cups rice
1/2 cup water
1/4 teaspoon saffron
1/4 teaspoon curry powder
1/4 teaspoon paprika

Prepare the shrimp:
Heat 1 tablespoon of olive oil over medium heat in a large saucepan. Sauté the shallots and garlic for 1 minute. Add the chopped tomatoes and cook over low heat until tender. Add the shrimp and sauté until tender.

Prepare the rice:
Sauté onion in 1 tablespoon of olive oil over medium heat for 10 minutes. Add rice and water and bring to a boil. Add saffron, curry powder, and paprika and reduce heat to low. Cover and simmer over low heat for 20 minutes, or until rice is tender.

Garnish with freshly chopped paprika and season with salt and pepper.

Tarte Tatin

EIGHT SERVINGS

For the Pastry:

1 cup unbleached all purpose flour
8 tablespoons unsalted butter
1/4 cup sugar
3 eggs, beaten
2 teaspoons water

For the Filling:

12 large, firm apples
14 tablespoons unsalted butter, cut into small pieces
1-1/2 cups sugar

Prepare the pastry:

Place the flour and butter in a food processor bowl and pulse to blend, about 5 seconds. Add the sugar and eggs and process until well blended, about 10 seconds. Add the water 1 tablespoon at a time and pulse until the mixture begins to form a ball.

Form the dough into a flattened round and chill, covered, for at least an hour.

Prepare the filling:

Preheat oven to 350°F. Peel and core the apples. Slice each apple lengthwise in 4 pieces. In a 9-inch tarte tatin pan or a cast-iron skillet, melt the butter over low heat. Add the sugar and cook until it turns a light caramel color.

Golden Delicious apples are ideal for this tarte tatin.

Beginning at the outside edge of the pan, place the apple slices along the edge of the pan with the rounded side down. Repeat with a second circle of apples inside the first. Fill in any gaps with the remaining apples. Bake for 1 hour until the apples soften and release their juices.

Assemble the tarte:

Roll the pastry out to form a 10-inch round. Put the pastry on top of the apples and bake for 20 – 30 minutes until the pastry is fully cooked. Immediately invert the tart onto a serving dish. Let cool slightly before slicing.

LA LANGOUSTE

Goat Cheese Salad

Provençale Fish Soup

Grilled Lobster, Sweet Potatoes and Rice

Banana Tart

FLAMANDS BEACH
SAINT BARTHÉLEMY, F.W.I.
05 90 27 63 61

As any person who has vacationed on the New England coast can attest, there is nothing quite like eating a lobster in an open air restaurant overlooking the ocean. The meal is simplicity itself, and the freshness of the lobster, combined with the sights, sounds and smells of being directly on the water, creates a memorable dining experience that keeps the faithful returning summer after summer.

La Langouste, also known as Annie's in tribute to its owner, Annie Ange, is such a place on St. Barths. Located directly on Flamands Beach in the Hotel Baie des Anges, also owned and managed by Annie, La Langouste serves fresh lobsters directly out of a large tank (the first of its kind on St. Barths) to the sound of waves rolling up on shore.

Annie is a member of the Turbe family which emigrated from Nantes in the Loire Valley in France to St. Barths in 1799. As is the custom among the older families on the island, the Turbes subdivided their extensive landholdings over the years and gave individual parcels to their children when they became adults.

In 1979, Annie was given the land on Flamands Beach where La Langouste presently sits. The following year, having worked for a number of restaurants on the island including Hotel Baie de Flamands (which was built by her brother on the land he received from their parents), Filao Beach and The Pelican, Annie opened her own restaurant in Gustavia called Annie's. It specialized in the simple island and Creole food that Annie had grown up eating and became very popular with locals including the police whose headquarters was nearby.

In 1982, she married her husband, Jean Pierre, who was a carpenter and builder, and together they set about the task of building the original hotel on her land in Flamands. The hotel consisted of two rows of traditional wooden cases facing one another across an open courtyard. It opened in 1984, and Annie assumed the added responsibilities of running the hotel and cooking breakfast for hotel guests while continuing to manage her restaurant in Gustavia.

In 1990, Annie opened a new restaurant in Gustavia and named it La Langouste in the hope that the name change would downplay her central role in the restaurant and free her from the necessity of being there every night. It didn't work. Her popularity remained as strong as ever, and the loyalty of her customers to her personally is such that to this day, over thirteen years after the

Annie Ange

name change, almost everyone continues to refer to La Langouste as Annie's.

In September of 1995, Hurricane Luis made short work of the hotel in Flamands, and Annie and Jean Pierre decided to replace it with a much larger hotel made of steel-reinforced concrete and move La Langouste from Gustavia to the hotel. The rebuilt hotel and restaurant opened on Valentine's Day in 1997. Annie's fear that the move to a more remote location in Flamands might affect the restaurant's popularity proved unfounded. Even the police from Gustavia continue to make regular visits to Annie's.

In its present incarnation, the restaurant is a comfortable place and overlooks the small terra cotta deck and hotel pool and the ocean beyond.

As reminiscent as La Langouste is of eating lobster in the United States, there are important distinctions as well. In the first place, there is a marked difference between Maine lobsters and their Caribbean cousins (known as spiny lobsters) which more than make up for their lack of claws with an abundance of meat in the tails providing a much larger quantity of edible lobster overall. They are served split open and grilled, which greatly simplifies the task of removing the meat and enhances their flavor. At La Langouste, lobsters are paired with basmati rice, pureed squash and baked plantains. Three sauces accompany the lobster: ginger and tomato, Creole and traditional clarified butter. While clearly the star of the show, lobsters at La Langouste share the stage with a full menu of appetizers and desserts as well as a variety of main dishes. Thus it is possible to precede your lobster with a warm goat cheese salad or a traditional soupe de poissons, finish with a fruit tarte for dessert or skip the lobster altogether if you are so inclined. The wine list offers a number of attractive, reasonably-priced wines.

When La Langouste first reopened, it was not uncommon to see Annie's children doing their homework at an unoccupied table with Annie alternating between serving guests and keeping a watchful eye on the young scholars. Because St. Barths does not have a high school, Annie's children, like many children on the island, moved back to France a few years ago with their father to complete their education, returning home each summer. That leaves Annie and the family dog, Flea Bag, to hold down the fort in Flamands, although Flea Bag is so advanced in age and his arthritis so pronounced that his assistance is more of a spiritual nature, and he spends most of his time napping on the bottom shelf of the bookcase in the sitting area just to the side of the dining room.

To see Annie managing the hotel and restaurant entirely on her own while her family is several thousand miles away in France is to understand why she and her restaurant will always remain synonymous in the hearts and minds of her devoted fans. She possesses all of the independence, self-confidence and competence of her ancestors while exuding warmth and hospitality. Nothing fazes her, and she is unfailingly friendly and delighted to see customers whether they are locals, regular visitors making their annual pilgrimage to her restaurant or newcomers. The character of this woman is best exemplified by the ritual which precedes every lobster dinner. After taking the customer's order, Annie walks over to the lobster tank, makes her selection and does not flinch as she pulls the lobster out of the tank and carries it wet, writhing and snapping to the customer for a pre-grilling inspection. She may very well be the only person on the island who has the courage to do this with her bare hands. (Most prefer using a long stick and lasso-type device). She is certainly the only one who does it looking as elegant as she does in the black dress and pearls she wears each evening. She is the kind of person it is easy to think of as a favorite neighbor and trusted friend which must be why people insist upon calling her and her restaurant by her first name and keep coming back year after year.

Goat Cheese Salad

SIX SERVINGS

This simple dish is one of the most popular starters at La Langouste.

7 ounces goat cheese, softened
2 slices bacon
1 tablespoon olive oil
2 tablespoons basil, chopped
6 phyllo sheets, thawed if frozen
3 tablespoons butter, melted

Cook bacon until crisp. Cool and crumble into small pieces. Combine goat cheese, bacon, oil olive and basil. Roll into a log and refrigerate.

Preheat oven to 400°F.
Cover stack of phyllo with a sheet of plastic wrap and a dampened towel. Put 1 phyllo sheet on a work surface and brush with melted butter, then top with 2 more sheets of phyllo, brushing each with melted butter.

Cut phyllo stack into 6 x 6 inch squares. Slice goat cheese log into 6 equal rounds. Place goat cheese in center of phyllo square and pull the phyllo up around the goat cheese to form a bundle, twisting at the top. Brush with melted butter. Repeat with the remaining phyllo and goat cheese forming 6 bundles. (Can be made 1 day ahead of time. Cover and chill.)

Bake phyllo bundles on a buttered baking sheet until golden, approximately 10 to 12 minutes. Serve with tossed salad.

Provençale Fish Soup

FOUR SERVINGS

For the Soup:

2 pounds assorted lean fish, including fish heads and bones
4 limes, juiced
1 clove garlic, minced
1 cup onion, diced
1 leek, white parts chopped
2 tomatoes, coarsely chopped
1 tablespoon olive oil
5 parsley springs
1/2 teaspoon thyme
4 potatoes, peeled and sliced into 1/4 inch rounds
2 carrots, chopped
1 teaspoon saffron

For the Rouille:

1 red bell pepper, roasted, peeled and chopped
1/2 jalapeno pepper, minced
3 cloves of garlic, minced
1 tablespoon lemon juice
1/3 cup olive oil
Salt and pepper to taste

French bread, thinly sliced and toasted
1/2 cup gruyère, finely shredded

Prepare the soup:

Combine the lime juice, garlic, 1 cup of water and salt and pepper. Pour mixture over the fish and chill for 30 minutes.

For a flavorful fish soup, be sure to use several different types of fish. Recommendations include sea bass, halibut, cod, red snapper, rockfish, porgy and grouper.

Heat oil in a large Dutch oven over medium heat. Sauté onions and leeks until tender, approximately 10 minutes. Add tomatoes and sauté an additional 5 minutes. Drain fish and add to Dutch oven along with herbs, remaining vegetables, saffron and 2 quarts of water. Simmer at a low boil for 45 minutes.

Remove 3 to 4 slices of the potato from the soup (set aside for the rouille). Process the remaining soup through a food mill. Season to taste with salt and pepper.

Prepare the rouille:

Combine peppers, garlic and reserved potatoes in a food processor and pulse to combine. Add lemon juice and, with the machine running, add oil in a stream and process until smooth. Season with salt and pepper.

Top toasted bread slices with a tablespoon of the rouille. Ladle soup into bowls and top each bowl with 3 toasts and some shredded gruyère cheese.

Grilled Lobster, Sweet Potatoes and Rice

FOUR SERVINGS

Although you might not have access to the wonderful *langoustes* (spiny lobsters) that are Annie's claim to fame, you can duplicate the grilled lobster experience with a Maine lobster. We recommend par-boiling the lobsters before you split them for grilling.

4 lobsters, 1-1/2 to 2 pounds each
6 tablespoons clarified butter, melted

For the Sauce Creole:

1/4 cup parsley, chopped
1/4 cup cilantro, chopped
2 cloves of garlic, minced
1 teaspoon chili pepper, minced
1/3 cup olive oil
Salt and pepper to taste

For the Tomato Vinaigrette

1 tomato, peeled, seeded and chopped
1 teaspoon ginger, minced
1/3 cup olive oil
1 teaspoon chili pepper, minced
Salt and pepper to taste

Prepare the sauces:
Combine all the ingredients of the sauce Creole. Let steep for 30 minutes. Combine the tomato vinaigrette ingredients in a blender or food processor and puree briefly.

Prepare the lobsters:
Bring a large pot of salted water to a boil. Boil lobsters, 2 at a time, for 5 minutes being sure to return water to a complete boil before boiling additional lobsters.

When lobsters are cool enough to handle, twist off claws. Remove pot from heat and submerge claws in hot water for 10 minutes. Split the tails lengthwise in half from head to end of tail with poultry scissors and a knife. Drain the claws.

Prepare a medium-hot grill. Grill claws, turning occasionally, until liquid bubbles at the open end, 5-6 minutes, and transfer to a plate. Brush tail meat with some clarified butter and grill, meat side down, for 3 minutes. Turn lobsters shell side down, baste with butter and sprinkle with salt and pepper. Cover grill and cook for an additional 3 to 5 minutes or until the meat in the thickest part of the tail turns opaque.

For the Sweet Potatoes:

1-1/2 pounds sweet potatoes
4 tablespoons butter
1/3 cup heavy cream
1/4 teaspoon cinnamon
1/8 teaspoon salt

For the Rice:

2 cups water
1 cup basmati rice
1 tablespoon olive oil

Prepare the sweet potatoes:
Place whole sweet potatoes in a large pot and add enough cold water to cover by 1 inch. Add salt and bring to a boil. Cover and boil until sweet potatoes can be easily pierced with a knife, approximately 20 - 30 minutes, depending on size. Drain potatoes and let cool. When potatoes are cool, remove the skins and force them through a food mill or ricer. Heat the cream and butter over medium heat until the butter is thoroughly melted. Add the cream mixture and cinnamon to the potatoes and whisk to combine.

Prepare the basmati rice:
Bring water, salt and olive oil to a boil. Add rice, cover and cook over low heat until all the water is absorbed, approximately 20 minutes. Let stand, covered, for 5 minutes before serving.

Serve lobsters with tomato vinaigrette, Creole sauce, clarified butter, rice and sweet potatoes.

Banana Tart

FOUR SERVINGS

2 tablespoons butter
1-1/2 tablespoons sugar
2 bananas, cut into 1/4-inch thick slices
1 sheet (about 1/2 pound) frozen puff pastry, thawed
2 tablespoons vanilla rum

Preheat the oven to 400°F.

Combine the butter and sugar in a heavy skillet over medium heat. Add the chopped bananas and cook until they are slightly browned.

Roll out the puff pastry on a lightly floured surface and cut out 4 rounds, each approximately 4 inches in diameter. Transfer the pastry to a baking sheet. Arrange the banana slices, overlapping them slightly, on the pastry rounds, covering the rounds completely.

Bake the banana tarts for 25 to 30 minutes, or until the pastry is golden brown.

Transfer the tarts to a rack, sprinkle them with vanilla rum and serve immediately.

MAYA'S

Tomato and Mango Salad

Shrimp Curry

Filet of Beef Creole

West Indian Orange Cake

PUBLIC
SAINT BARTHÉLEMY, F.W.I.
05 90 27 75 73

People who return to the same place for vacation each year often develop customs which act as a bridge of sorts spanning what can seem like an interminable wait between visits. They idle away the months by visualizing and reliving the details from past vacations and take comfort in the knowledge that those very same experiences await them on their return. In St. Barths, these rituals take many forms. For some, it is buying a couple of Caribs with wedges of lime upon arrival in St. Maarten while awaiting the short flight which is the last leg of their journey. For others, it is making a detour to Saline immediately after landing on the island for a quick swim before the sun sets or the first trip to the Match for a crusty baguette, cheese and a bottle of wine. The list is as long and varied as the number of people who return to the island each year, but for many it includes at least one trip to Maya's restaurant just outside Gustavia in Public.

Randy and Maya Gurley opened Maya's nearly twenty years ago. Like a number of other people involved in St. Barths' culinary world, the idea of running a restaurant evolved gradually for Randy and Maya from a series of life experiences which made taking the plunge into the food business a promising but by no means foregone conclusion. Maya was born in Martinique and raised in Guadeloupe as part of a very large family which included thirteen children on her father's side of the family, six on her mother's side and a total of thirty-five first cousins. Despite its size, the family was very close-knit. Many of the children, including Maya, were educated in France where they lived with their grandmother who moved to France from Guadeloupe for the express purpose of taking care of the children while they finished their studies. The family loved to get together for all kinds of occasions, and they loved to eat.

Maya's husband, Randy, was born 1600 miles to the north on the island of Nantucket and, like generations of Nantucket natives before him, was drawn to the sea. Accordingly, after graduating from college in 1976, he sailed his family's forty-five foot sloop to Antigua to begin a charter business and divided his time between the Caribbean in the winter and the waters of coastal New England in the summer. One of his earliest charters was from Antigua to St. Barths. Upon arriving in Gustavia, he became so enamored of the place that he decided to make it his home port in the winter and lived on his boat at various anchorages around the island. He met Maya shortly thereafter who was staying at the Emeraude Plage Hotel

Randy Gurley, Chef Eddy Coquin and Maya Gurley

and juggling a variety of jobs which included waitressing and cooking at the restaurant in the hotel as well as working as a draftswoman for a local architect. Randy offered Maya a job crewing on his next charter from Antigua, and she accepted.

Unhappily for the passengers but luckily for Randy and Maya, the wind died and the engine conked out somewhere between Antigua and Guadeloupe, which left the boat becalmed and drifting aimlessly for several days but gave the skipper and his newly-hired crew member time to become better acquainted. It also provided an opportunity for Maya to demonstrate a talent which is very much in evidence to this day. Specifically, with provisions

running low, Maya rummaged around the galley and concocted what Randy still remembers as an extraordinary meal from the kinds of rations – condensed milk and canned vegetables and meat – which are consumed by sailors only in dire emergencies. Shortly thereafter, Maya took up residence with Randy on the boat which was their home for nearly eight years and joined him on charters throughout the Caribbean and New England.

In 1983, Randy and Maya had their first child and decided to establish a more permanent existence on St. Barths. They built a house later that year and, encouraged by years of Maya's triumphs as a galley chef in the charter business, bought a restaurant the following summer which was located on the land on which Maya's presently sits but was much smaller and had the dubious distinction of being illuminated with green neon lights which were so bright that they could be seen on Nevis. It was furnished with brown picnic tables, and the kitchen had a single oven and a dirt floor. The Gurleys expanded the dining area and laid down flooring for it as well as the kitchen. They did extensive landscaping around the outside of the restaurant including the attractive rock garden to the rear of the dining area. They also stripped the restaurant of its unfortunate lighting fixtures and furnishings and replaced them with soft lighting, colorful director's chairs, embroidered placemats and napkins and simple wooden tables made by Randy and a friend on St. Barths – all of which remain in use today.

Upon entering Maya's, the visitor is greeted by the buzz of diners who are having a good time. There is also the sense of intimacy which exists in well loved restaurants. Many of the patrons at Maya's have been here before, are seated at their favorite tables and ordering their favorite meals and are clearly relishing the opportunity to spend another evening with Randy and Maya. Randy works the front of the restaurant with an easy affability greeting old friends and newcomers alike in fluent French as well as English. Maya makes a point of escaping from the kitchen at various times throughout the evening to catch up with her many friends. The waitstaff is chosen and trained with care as evidenced by uniformly excellent service.

The food, like the décor, is simplicity itself. Due in no small part to Maya having been raised in Guadeloupe, Maya's was one of the first restaurants on St. Barths to find inspiration in the culinary traditions of the Caribbean rather than France. Fresh ingredients drive the menu at Maya's, and specials change daily. When the restaurant first opened, Maya's quest for the very best produce led her to pay a visit each morning to a stall in Gustavia run by women from Guadeloupe who sailed to St. Barths each week with a new shipment of fruits and vegetables. Maya continues this practice today.

Maya and Randy had a modest-sounding but inspired goal when they opened their restaurant: they wanted to serve good food in comfortable surroundings that felt much like the meals Maya shared with her many aunts, uncles and cousins. They have met this goal and continue to do so, and Maya's has thus become a fixture in the vacations of many people who return to St. Barths each year.

Tomato and Mango Salad

FOUR SERVINGS

This colorful salad is a favorite at Maya's, and is at its best when prepared with ripe, farm fresh tomatoes.

Make the vinaigrette:
In a small bowl whisk together vinegar, mustard, and shallots. Add olive in a stream, whisking, until vinaigrette has emulsified. Season to taste with salt and pepper.

Assemble the salad:
Peel and slice the mangoes. Slice the tomatoes and arrange in an overlapping circle with the mango slices on a plate. Garnish with chives and basil and top with the vinaigrette.

For the Vinaigrette:
3 tablespoons balsamic vinegar
1 teaspoon Dijon mustard
1 small shallot, minced
Salt and pepper to taste
1/2 cup extra-virgin olive oil

For the Salad:
2 large, ripe tomatoes
2 large mangoes
2 tablespoons freshly chopped chives
2 tablespoons fresh basil, cut into a chiffonade

To create a basil chiffonade, make a small stack of basil leaves and roll tightly into a cylinder. Slice the cylinder of leaves crosswise into thin strips.

Shrimp Curry

FOUR SERVINGS

24 large shrimp
1-1/2 cups water
2 tablespoons corn oil
1 onion, diced
3 tablespoons red curry paste
1 cup coconut milk
1 hot chili pepper, finely diced

Peel and devein the shrimp, reserving the shells. Simmer the shells in 1-1/2 cups of water for 15 minutes over medium heat. Pass the shrimp broth through a sieve and discard shells.

Heat the corn oil in a medium skillet over moderate heat. Add the onion and cook until just tender, approximately 10 minutes. Add the curry paste and 1/4 cup shrimp broth and cook for 5 minutes. Add 1/2 of the coconut milk and simmer for an additional 5 minutes, slowly adding remaining coconut milk. Season to taste with salt, pepper and desired amount of chili pepper.

Add shrimp to the sauce and poach the shrimp until just cooked through, approximately 3 to 4 minutes. Serve shrimp and curry sauce over white rice.

Filet of Beef Creole

FOUR SERVINGS

The French cut of beef known as the filet is more commonly referred to as the tenderloin in the United States. The meat tastes best when cooked rare.

2 to 3 pound filet of beef (beef tenderloin), trimmed and tied

For the Marinade:

2/3 cup olive oil
1/4 cup white wine vinegar
1/4 cup red wine vinegar
1 tablespoon fresh thyme leaves
2 teaspoons red chili pepper, seeded and minced
3 cloves garlic, minced
2 tablespoons freshly chopped chives
Salt and pepper to taste

Combine all of the marinade ingredients. Set aside 1/3 cup of the marinade.

In a resealable bag, combine 2/3 of the marinade and the filet. Turn the bag to be certain the meat is thoroughly coated. Chill filet and marinate for at least 15 minutes and up to 8 hours. Let filet stand at room temperature for 30 minutes before grilling.

Prepare a very hot grill.

Grill filet over high heat for approximately 20 to 25 minutes, turning every 5 minutes, until a meat thermometer registers 125°F to 130°F for rare. Transfer to platter and let stand for 10 minutes.

Bring the remaining marinade to a boil over high heat. Reduce heat and simmer the marinade while the filet is resting. Slice the filet and served with the warm marinade.

West Indian Orange Cake

EIGHT SERVINGS

This traditional West Indian orange cake gets its intense flavor from the fresh orange zest and is delicious when paired with vanilla rum.

- 1 cup (2 sticks) unsalted butter
- 1-1/2 cups sugar
- Zest of four oranges
- 5 large egg yolks
- 3 cups flour
- 1 teaspoon baking powder
- 1/2 teaspoon baking soda
- 1 cup orange juice
- 4 large egg whites

Preheat oven to 375°F.

Cream the butter, sugar and orange zest until fluffy. Mix in one egg yolk at a time. In a large bowl, mix together the flour, baking powder, and baking soda. Alternating between the dry ingredients and the orange juice, gradually add both to the butter mixture, mixing well.

Beat the egg whites until they form stiff peaks. Fold 1/3 of the egg whites into the batter to lighten it and then gently fold in the remaining whites.

Pour batter into a greased 9-inch tube pan. Bake for 50 minutes or until a toothpick inserted in the top comes out clean.

NEW BORN

Conch Gratin

Mahi Mahi with Sauce Vert

Red Snapper in Court Bouillon

Banana Flambé

ANSE DES CAYES
SAINT BARTHÉLEMY, F.W.I.
05 90 27 67 07

To say Franckie Greaux greeted the idea of being included in a restaurant book about St. Barths with skepticism is a gross understatement. Along with his brother, David, Franckie runs New Born Restaurant out of what is still the ground floor of his parents' home in Anse des Cayes and has never felt the slightest inclination or need to promote his restaurant in any way. New Born isn't so much of a commercial enterprise as an extension of what the Greaux family has been doing for fourteen generations in St. Barths: starting each day catching fresh fish ranging from red snapper, rock grouper, mahi mahi, bonita, wahoo, tiger shark and lobster and concluding with a delicious home-cooked meal.

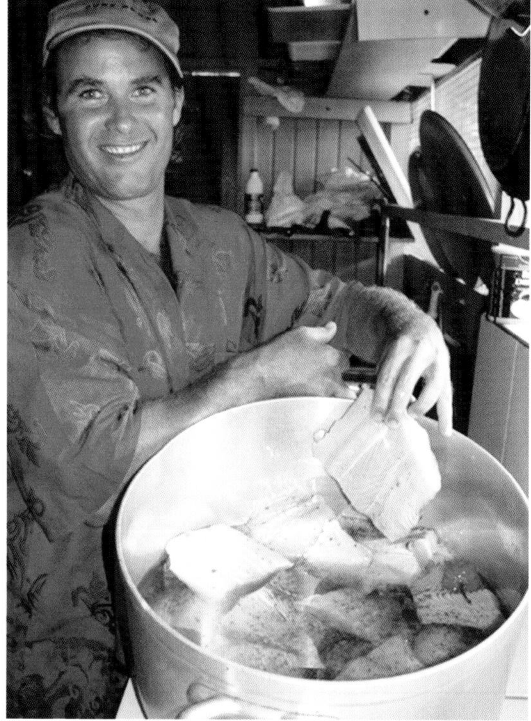

Franckie Greaux

Asking Franckie when he began fishing is like asking him when he began to breathe. Fishing is so integral to Franckie's life, and fishing the waters off St. Barths in particular, that it is impossible to imagine him doing anything else. And the same is true for David. When asked whether he had always fished with David, Franckie flashed the same slightly puzzled and bemused smile with which he had reacted to the idea of the book and said "of course" as though there was no other conceivable way either of them could have spent their time. They may, in fact, be part amphibian judging from the stories Franckie tells of being able to do free dives to a depth of twenty-two meters when he was younger, armed with a spear gun in search of quarry like stingrays, a feat which Franckie concedes he can only accomplish now at a depth of fifteen meters due to the combined effects of age and tobacco.

The typical workday for Franckie and David begins at 5:30 a.m. when they head out in one of their two boats into the waters surrounding St. Barths and St. Maarten with occasional trips as far as sixty miles out to sea. As anyone who has sailed in this part of the world knows, the pictures of placid inlets ringed by palm trees and white sand beaches tell only a part of the story about boating conditions in the Caribbean, and a small part of the story at that. Strong winds, large swells and white-capped waves are a common occurrence and make fishing these waters very hard work indeed.

A lifetime of experience has taught Franckie and David precisely where and under what conditions – seasons, tides, temperatures, weather and phases of the moon – to find particular fish. They also employ ingenious methods for catching fish such as floating plastic mesh nets on the surface of the water to provide a dark sanctuary for small fish which, in turn, attract the larger fish. They are very respectful of the fact that fish are a finite resource and accordingly eschew the use of nets which sweep up large numbers of unwanted fish indiscriminately and opt instead to rely upon a hook and line, catching one fish at a time. On any given day, they also run approximately a hundred lobster traps which they make and repair themselves. Employing a technique that could only have been devised by the French, Franckie and David leave female lobsters with eggs in the traps not only to preserve their ability to perpetuate the species but to harness the power of their seductive charms and lure unwitting male lobsters into captivity.

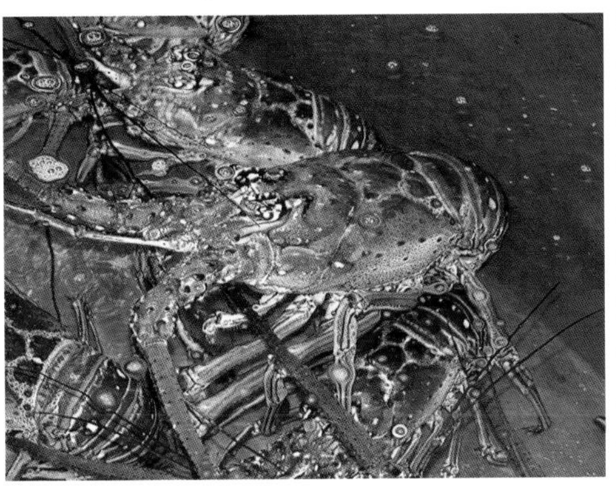

By mid-morning, Franckie and David return home with that day's catch. The fish are cleaned in preparation for dinner; the lobsters are placed in a large tank which is continuously fed by water pumped directly from the ocean. Certain fish – shark, wahoo and bonito – are smoked for two days in a smokehouse built by Franckie and served as one of the most delectable appetizers on St. Barths. A large aquarium dominates one of the walls in the dining room and is filled with fish who have been spared being used as bait or served for dinner including a large grouper to whom Franckie refers fondly as "the old guy."

It is then time for the brothers to clean up and get ready for dinner. Over the course of an evening, a number of guests will arrive on foot as New Born

David and Franckie Greaux

is very much of a neighborhood place. This is not to suggest, however, that the American arriving by car from a different part of the island feels even the slightest bit out of place. To the contrary, Franckie and David greet all visitors as friends and make them feel right at home. Given the hospitality of people on St. Barths, as well as the friendliness and informality of New Born in particular, it is not uncommon for conversations to arise among diners at different tables, locals and vacationers alike.

Their mother, Agnes, presides in the kitchen with Franckie and David filling in when necessary. When not driving his taxi, their father cooks lobsters over an outdoor wood grill. None of the recipes which appear in this book from New Born were written down. Agnes cooks from memory based upon years of experience and lessons passed down from generation to generation. The only way to learn New Born's recipes is to watch Agnes at work and then savor the fruits of her labors.

With characteristic yet excessive modesty, Franckie states that you "don't have to be a magician" to cook the food at New Born. The emphasis is on freshness and simplicity. Franckie is passionate about the lobster and fish he serves and will eagerly display samples of his daily catch to curious guests. One evening, Franckie proudly carried a tray full of red snapper around the dining room. The eyes of the fish were as clear as crystals, and the skin glistened with the briny vitality of the sea. Someone mentioned how good one feels after eating fresh fish. Franckie fairly beamed at this statement, taking it not so much as a personal compliment as an affirmation of one of the fundamental truths in his life, a life he and the Greaux family are happy to share at New Born.

Conch Gratin

FOUR SERVINGS

1 pound fresh conch, cleaned
2 tablespoons chopped parsley
1 teaspoon fresh thyme
1 small onion, diced
1/4 cup chopped scallions, white parts only
2 cloves garlic, minced
1 cup fresh bread crumbs
1/2 cup Gruyère cheese, grated

Garnish: scallop shells

This dish is also delicious when made with fresh clams.

Preheat oven to 400°F.

Slice the conch into small pieces. Place the conch pieces in a medium saucepan, add enough water to cover and simmer over moderate heat for 20 minutes. Add parsley, thyme, onions, scallions and garlic and continue simmering until sauce reduces and thickens.

Toast bread crumbs on a cookie sheet in the oven for 5 minutes or until just brown.

Remove conch mixture from heat and stir in bread crumbs. Divide conch mixture between 6 buttered scallop shells (or ramekins) and top with grated cheese. Broil until cheese melts.

Mahi Mahi with Sauce Vert

FOUR SERVINGS

Prepare a medium-hot charcoal fire or preheat a gas grill.

Rinse fish and pat dry. Mix together all ingredients for sauce vert. Combine 1/3 sauce vert with lemon juice and coat filets using a brush. Place filets skin side down on grill. Grill for 8 minutes, turning carefully halfway through grilling.

Heat remaining sauce vert and serve with grilled fish.

4 mahi mahi filets

For the Sauce Vert:

6 tablespoons olive oil
6 scallions, white parts chopped
2 cloves garlic, minced
6 tablespoons parsley, chopped
1 medium onion, diced
1/4 teaspoon chopped bonnet chili
1/4 teaspoon salt
1/4 teaspoon pepper
2 teaspoons lemon juice

Red Snapper in Court Bouillon

TWO SERVINGS

2 whole red snappers, cleaned, leaving heads and tails intact
1/2 scotch bonnet chili, seeded and chopped
4 tablespoons olive oil
1 cup diced onion
1/4 cup chopped parsley
5-6 scallions, white parts chopped
6 sprigs thyme
2 cloves garlic, minced
1 cup chopped tomatoes
1 tablespoon tomato paste
1/4 teaspoon salt

Court bouillon is French for "quick broth" and is a traditional method of poaching seafood. You can substitute any whole fish that is a similar size, such as striped bass, for the red snapper in this recipe.

Combine scotch bonnet chili with 2 tablespoons of olive oil and set aside. Heat remaining olive oil in a 4 -6 quart heavy saucepan (large enough to hold both fish) and sauté onions until golden over medium heat, approximately 10 minutes. Add parsley, scallions, thyme, garlic and 1 teaspoon of the hot pepper olive oil and sauté for 2 minutes. Gradually add chopped tomatoes, stirring constantly. Stir in tomato paste and add the fish. Add salt and 2 cups of water. Increase heat to medium-high and simmer, covered, for 10 minutes.

Transfer fish with a slotted spoon to plate and spoon court bouillon over the fish. Serve immediately.

Banana Flambé

TWO SERVINGS

4 tablespoons rum
2 tablespoons banana liquor
4 teaspoons brown sugar
1 tablespoon water
2 teaspoons butter
1 tablespoon cinnamon
2 bananas, peeled and sliced lengthwise and in half
Vanilla ice cream

In a small sauce pan, combine the rum and banana liquor and cook over moderate heat for 2 minutes.

In a separate saucepan, heat the brown sugar and water over medium heat, stirring constantly, until the sugar dissolves. Add the butter, cinnamon and sliced bananas and sauté for 5 minutes. Remove the pan from the heat and pour the rum and banana liquor over the bananas. Carefully ignite. Serve immediately with vanilla ice cream.

LE SAPOTILLIER

Frog's Legs

Squab Stuffed with Foie Gras

Duck Confit

Raspberry Soufflé

GUSTAVIA
SAINT BARTHÉLEMY, F.W.I.
05 90 27 60 28

Dining out in good restaurants is undoubtedly one of life's great pleasures. At its most basic level, it represents a break from the daily routine of having to purchase, prepare and clean up after meals. It also broadens culinary tastes and horizons. Perhaps most importantly, however, it provides an opportunity for people to spend a couple of hours together, talk and reconnect.

Every once in a while, one discovers a restaurant where the setting is so pretty, the service so gracious and the food so good that it elevates the dining experience to the level of the sublime and, in so doing, transports those lucky enough to be there to a plane where dinner conversation and dining companions sparkle and glitter like diamonds. Le Sapotillier is such a restaurant.

Le Sapotillier is an intimate place located a few doors down from the Anglican Church in Gustavia. It is divided into three small dining areas: the elegant stone-walled room in front as you enter the restaurant; a traditional Caribbean wood frame structure; and an outdoor terrace which connects the two where the sapotillier tree from which the restaurant derived its name used to grow before it was destroyed in a hurricane. The menu features French classics which have long been the stuff of romance: seared foie gras, frog's legs, duck confit, squab, and soufflés lighter than air. The wine list is impressive. And the waitstaff are warm, attentive and unobtrusive.

The heart and soul of Le Sapotillier is its owner, Adam Rajner, who personally greets everyone entering the restaurant with the words: "Bon soir. My name is Adam, and this is my restaurant." He says this not out of any sense of self importance but rather to assure his guests that he has looked after every detail and spared no effort to provide as memorable a dining experience as possible. It is Adam who shows diners to their tables, explains the menu, takes their orders, and returns at various points throughout the meal to make certain that everything is to their satisfaction. He is passionate about the quality of the ingredients used in his food. For example, he uses only certain kinds of apples in his tarts which have been harvested precisely at the right moment to give them the requisite sourness and alters his menu to accommodate the subtle variations in the taste of goat cheese from season to season. He imports most of his food from France, including the highly prized Bresse chickens from a region northeast of Lyons, even though it is more difficult and expensive to do so. His relationships

Adam and Nicole Rajner

with suppliers, many of which are small, family-run operations which no longer accept new customers, go back thirty years, and he visits them each year on return trips to France. Adam and his wife Nicole eat dinner every night with the staff and discuss how to fine tune and improve upon the prior evening's dining experience. Adam notes that the word restaurant comes from the word restore, and he is deeply committed to making certain that dinner at Le Sapotillier fulfills this important function.

Adam's immense personal charm, and, by extension, the charm of Le Sapotillier, cannot be fully understood or appreciated, however, without knowing more about his past and what brought him to St. Barths over seventeen years ago. A native of Hungary and born into a family which had lost everything to the Nazis in World War II, Adam fled his home in 1956 when Soviet troops brutally suppressed the nascent Hungarian independence movement. He studied hotel and restaurant management in Vienna and worked in France and England for a number of years before moving to Nice where he owned and operated a successful brasserie for the next fifteen years. When the socialists and communists swept into power in France in the early 1980's, however, Adam promptly put his brasserie on the market and began looking for somewhere else to work and live. He sold the brasserie on October 14, 1985 and bought Le Sapotillier – sight unseen – a couple of days later.

Le Sapotillier opened on November 11, 1985. In explaining his decision to uproot his family and move them thousands of miles to a part of the world they had never even visited, Adam says that there are moments in life where you know in your heart what is right; when your conscience knows what your mind does not. Like many others in St. Barths, he decided to listen to his heart and go where it told him to go. He has never regretted his decision.

For many people, hard work is endless drudgery. For Adam, the opportunity to work hard and to excel is a privilege and a gift. Le Sapotillier is a testament to Adam's lifelong pursuit of independence and personal freedom, and his loyal patrons are the lucky beneficiaries.

Frog's Legs

FOUR SERVINGS

Frog's legs have a delicate, subtle flavor and do, in fact, taste quite a lot like chicken. Fresh frog's legs are generally available from April through the end of the summer at gourmet markets and fish stores.

Mix together the garlic, chopped parsley and olive oil. Thoroughly coat the frog's legs with the parsley mixture and marinate for several hours. Heat the clarified butter over relatively high heat in a large skillet. Add the frog's legs and sauté for 3 - 4 minutes, until they are nicely brown. Season with salt and pepper and serve immediately.

24 frog's legs
3 cloves garlic, minced
3/4 cup chopped fresh parsley
1 tablespoon olive oil
2 tablespoons clarified butter
Sea salt and freshly ground pepper to taste

Squab Stuffed with Foie Gras

FOUR SERVINGS

4 squab (10-1/2 – 12 ounces each)

For the Red Wine Gravy:

1 tablespoon olive oil
1 medium shallot, chopped
1/2 teaspoon fresh thyme leaves
2 cups red wine
7 cloves
1 cinnamon stick

For the Stuffing:

1/2 tablespoon duck fat or butter
1 shallot, chopped
1/2 cup cooked chicken (white meat), diced
8 ounces foie gras, cut into small pieces
Salt and pepper to taste

For the Spaetzle:

1/2 cup cold milk
1/4 cup heavy cream
3 large eggs
1 teaspoon salt
1/4 teaspoon ground nutmeg
2 cups all purpose flour

Squab is a dark meat bird that is extremely succulent. For the most flavorful meat, it should be served medium-rare, when the juices run pink.

Prepare the red wine sauce:
Preheat the oven to 400°F. Debone the squab and refrigerate, reserving the bones. In a medium roasting pan, roast the bones until just browned, approximately 5 minutes. Add enough water to cover the bones and simmer for 30 minutes. Strain stock through a fine sieve and discard bones.

Heat the olive oil over moderate heat in a medium saucepan. Add the shallots and thyme and sauté over medium heat until the shallots soften, about 3 minutes. Add the reserved stock, wine, cloves and cinnamon and simmer over medium heat until reduced to 3/4 cup. Strain sauce.

Prepare the stuffing:
Sauté the shallots in the duck fat or butter over medium heat until soft, approximately 5 minutes. Let the shallots cool and then mix them together with the diced chicken, foie gras, salt and pepper.

Prepare the spaetzle:
Whisk together the milk, cream, eggs, salt and nutmeg in a large bowl. Add flour and blend until batter is just smooth (batter will be quite sticky). Bring large pot of salted water to slow boil. Working in batches, pour batter through a spaetzle maker into the boiling water (alternatively work the

batter through a large slotted spoon). Simmer for 2 minutes. Using a slotted spoon, transfer the spaetzle to large buttered baking dish. Toss with melted butter and season to taste with salt and pepper.

Make the squab:
Preheat oven to 450°F. Evenly fill the squab with the stuffing mixture and truss the birds. Heat 1 tablespoon of olive oil in a heavy sauté pan and brown squabs on all sides, approximately 5 minutes total. Season with salt and pepper and place the squab on their side in a medium roasting pan. Roast in the oven for 5 minutes. Turn to the other side and roast for 5 additional minutes. Lastly, turn squab breast side up and roast for 10 additional minutes or until an instant read thermometer reads 140°F. Remove from oven and let rest for 5 minutes. Reheat the red wine sauce. Serve squab on spaetzle with red wine sauce and braised red cabbage.

Duck Confit

FOUR SERVINGS

For the Duck Confit:

4 duck legs with thighs
2 duck breasts, split
3 tablespoons salt
2 tablespoons fresh thyme leaves
2 bay leaves, crumbled
4 cloves garlic, minced
About 6 cups duck fat

For the Red Wine Sauce:

2 cups red wine
1 teaspoon sugar
2 tablespoons butter
1/8 teaspoon salt
1/8 teaspoon pepper

Prepare the duck confit:
Combine the salt, thyme, bay leaves and garlic and coat duck pieces with mixture. Cover and refrigerate for 1-2 days.

Melt the duck fat in a pot large enough to hold the duck pieces. Rinse the duck pieces, pat dry and carefully submerge them in the melted fat. Cook, uncovered, over very low heat (the fat should not exceed 200°F) until the duck is tender and can be easily pulled from the bone, 2-3 hours. Remove the duck pieces with a slotted spoon and strain the fat through a fine sieve. Return the duck pieces to the pot and cover with the strained fat. Refrigerate for 3 hours.

For the best flavor, store the duck in the fat for at least 2 weeks and up to 2 months.

To use, remove duck from the fat. Pan sear in a hot skillet, skin side down, for 5 minutes. Turn and cook an additional 2 minutes.

Prepare the red wine sauce:
Combine the red wine and sugar and bring to a boil. Cook at a low boil until liquid is reduced to 3/4 cup. Remove from heat and whisk in butter, 1 tablespoon at a time. Season with salt and pepper.

Raspberry Soufflé

FOUR SERVINGS

For the Crème Pâtissière:

1/2 cup granulated sugar
2-1/2 egg yolks
1/4 cup flour
1 cup boiling milk
1/2 tablespoon butter
3/4 tablespoon vanilla extract

For the Soufflé:

2 tablespoons butter, softened
4 ounces raspberries
10 ounces egg whites
1/8 teaspoon cream of tarter
2 tablespoons sugar plus additional for coating ramekins

6 1-cup ramekins

The key to a successful soufflé is careful preparation of the beaten egg whites. For the best results, let the eggs whites sit at room temperature for 15 - 20 minutes and beat them in a unlined copper or stainless steel bowl.

Le Sapotillier uses a traditional pastry cream base, or crème pâtissière, in its soufflés.

Prepare the crème pâtissière:
Beat the sugar into the egg yolks and continue beating for 2 to 3 minutes until the mixture is pale yellow. Beat in the flour. Gradually pour the boiling milk in a thin stream into the yolk mixture, beating constantly. Pour into a saucepan and whisk over moderately high heat. Bring to a boil, reduce heat to medium-low, and continue to cook, whisking, for 3 additional minutes. Remove from the heat and beat in the butter and vanilla extract. Crème pâtissière will keep for a week in the refrigerator or it may be frozen.

Prepare the soufflé:
Preheat the oven to 375°F and prepare the ramekins by brushing them with softened (not melted) butter and sprinkling them with sugar so that the inside is thoroughly coated. Tap out the excess sugar.

Combine raspberries with crème pâtissière. Beat the egg whites with cream of tartar and a pinch of salt until they hold soft peaks. Add 2 tablespoons of sugar, beating until whites hold stiff peaks and are roughly 7 to 8 times their original volume. Fold 1/3 of the egg whites into the raspberry mixture to lighten it. Gently fold in remaining whites.

Divide soufflé mixture among ramekins and bake in lower third of oven for 17 to 20 minutes. Serve immediately.

HOSTELLERIE
des
3 FORCES

TROIS FORCES

Fish Quenelles

Curried Escargot

Châteaubriand with Peppercorn Sauce

Profiteroles with Chocolate Sauce

VITET
SAINT BARTHÉLEMY, F.W.I.
05 90 27 61 25

The guiding philosophy of Hubert De La Motte, which informs everything he does, is that all human activity should be dedicated to channeling as much positive energy into life as possible. Hubert has found many outlets for this simple yet powerful credo including the services he provides as an astrologer and spiritual adviser.

He is also a hotelier who offers visitors to St. Barths a sanctuary free from modern distractions like telephones and television in eight airy and pleasant cottages arrayed on a hillside in Vitet. Guests of the hotel are welcome to avail themselves of as much or little of Hubert's holistic services as they wish. Like everything else on St. Barths, Hubert's approach to these activities is relaxed and understated.

Finally, and to the great good fortune of those in search of a meal, Hubert is a chef. A sign reading "Food is Love" is prominently displayed in his restaurant. To Hubert, this represents both the emotional investment required to create great food as well as the effect that a meal which has been lovingly prepared has on those who consume it. And he should know: he is one of the longest-reigning chefs on St. Barths, and he has been working culinary magic since he began cooking on the island nearly twenty years ago.

Hubert first visited St. Barths in 1979. Having trained at what was then the two Michelin-starred Auberge du Vent Galant in Paris (which opened in the fifteenth century during the reign of Henry IV) as well as in kitchens in England, Scotland and Germany, he was working for a cruise ship which had docked in Gustavia. Hubert distinctly remembers looking out of one of the windows of the ship while polishing glasses and silverware, being mesmerized by the light and mountains in the distance, and feeling spiritually drawn to the island. As a man who very much knows his mind about such matters, Hubert decided right then and there that he would spend the rest of his life on St. Barths. He made the move a couple of years later.

Hubert and Ginette De La Motte

Shortly after taking up residency, he spotted a local girl named Ginette driving a taxi who, as Hubert describes it, was "stuck in paradise" and knew in an instant that she would be his wife despite never having met her. In his pleasantly forthright manner, Hubert announced this fact to the startled Ginette who laughed at the audacity of such a prediction from a total stranger and walked away. They got married a year later and began construction of Trois Forces which opened in 1984.

The menu at Trois Forces is classically French – more so than at any other restaurant on St. Barths – and features such staples of the French kitchen as escargots, frog's legs and beef au poivre. Because of the consistently high demand for traditional French food, Hubert has made relatively few changes to the menu over the years and jokingly boasts that he has "been making the same mistakes for over twenty years." He is amazingly efficient and runs the entire restaurant with only Ginette's assistance in the kitchen. It is therefore Hubert who welcomes diners to Trois Forces, explains the menu, advises about the choice of wine from a wine list which is notable both for its quality and reasonable prices and takes orders. He then rushes off to the kitchen where he cooks each meal individually (he even makes fresh pasta – admittedly not French but popular with certain customers nonetheless – on an order-by-order basis) returning to serve the meal, keep wines glasses filled and spend time with his guests.

In addition to being the dean of the St. Barths culinary world, Hubert is also one of its most highly decorated chefs. In 1993, he received the Diplome D'Honneur and Gold Medal from the Confrerie Gastronomique de la Marmite d'Or, formerly known as the Ancienne Compagnie Royale des Officiers de Bouche, which was established in 1657 as France's first food academy. In 2000, he was named the organization's District Governor for the French West Indies and in that capacity is responsible for overseeing educational activities and the preservation and promotion of French cooking in Martinique, Guadeloupe and St. Maarten as well as St. Barths. (The chef at Le Bec Fin in Philadelphia recently received the same award in recognition of his contributions to the advancement of French cuisine in the United States).

As befits someone of his training and experience, Hubert is a veritable encyclopedia of information about French food and can describe the origins of virtually ever item on his menu. Jonathan Swift wrote that "he was a bold man that first ate an oyster." Whether he was bold or not, he was certainly hungry, and the same explanation exists for many French dishes. For example. Hubert pointed out that the escargots and frog's legs which are so popular at Trois Forces were first consumed by peasants who had been forced to give all of the traditional food they raised to the nobles. Necessity being the mother of invention, the peasants devised ingenious ways to season and cook such unconventional ingredients making them not only edible but delicious in the process. The nobles, in turn, could not help but notice the strange and wonderful aromas emanating from the exotic food being prepared by the peasants and demanded a taste. And voila! French cuisine was born.

Desserts are also traditional and made to order. Perhaps no dessert captures the mood of Trois Forces better than the profiteroles which Hubert shapes into delicate swans. He positions the swans on the plate so that they appear to be kissing, and the graceful curve of their necks forms – what else? – a heart. Love is in the air at Trois Forces, and Hubert couldn't be more pleased.

Fish Quenelles

FOUR SERVINGS

For the Panade:

1/2 cup water
1/2 teaspoon salt
2 tablespoons butter
1/3 cup flour
1 egg
1 egg white

For the Quenelles:

1/3 pound skinless and boneless fish filets, cut into 1 inch pieces and chilled
1 tablespoon finely minced shallot
1 tablespoon chopped dill
1/4 teaspoon salt
1/8 teaspoon pepper
4 - 6 tablespoons heavy cream

For the Hollandaise Sauce:

3 egg yolks
1 1/2 tablespoons cold water
1/2 cup warm clarified butter
1 - 2 tablespoons fresh lemon juice
1/4 teaspoon salt
Pinch of salt and pepper

Quenelles are light, delicate dumplings that have a mousse-like texture. Hubert pairs the quenelles with a traditional Hollandaise sauce.

Prepare the panade:
Combine the water, salt and butter in a medium saucepan. Bring the water to a boil and stir to melt the butter. Remove from the heat and, using a wooden spoon, beat in the flour. Return the saucepan to the stove and continue to beat the mixture over medium-high heat until the mixture forms a thick paste. Remove from the heat and beat in the egg and the egg whites. Chill the panade completely.

Make the quenelles:
Place the fish filet pieces in a food processor fitted with a metal blade and process briefly. Add the chilled panade, shallots, dill, salt, pepper and 2 tablespoons of heavy cream and process for 30 seconds, scraping down the side of the bowl as necessary. Process in additional cream, 1 tablespoon at a time, being sure that the mixture continues to hold its shape.

The best fish quenelles are made with fish that have slightly gelatinous flesh, such as monkfish or halibut. The quenelles at Trois Forces are made with strawberry grouper.

Fit a pastry bag with a 1/2-inch tip and fill with the quenelle mixture. Squeeze out 2 inch long tubes.

In a large skillet, bring 3 inches of water to a low simmer. Carefully add the quenelles and poach until they have doubled in size, approximately 15 to 20 minutes. Remove with a slotted spoon and drain on a plate lined with a paper towel.

Make the hollandaise sauce:
Fill the bottom half of a double boiler with about 1-1/2 inches of water and bring to a low simmer. In the top half of a double boiler (off the heat), beat the egg yolks and water for 1 minute. Place the top of the double boiler over the barely simmering water and continue whisking the eggs until thickened, approximately 2 to 4 minutes. Remove the pan from the heat and whisk to cool slightly. Drop by drop, slowly add the clarified butter, whisking constantly. Whisk in the lemon juice, salt and pepper and serve immediately with the quenelles on a warm plate.

Curried Escargot

FOUR SERVINGS

1 8-ounce can escargot, drained
1 tablespoon butter
1/4 cup dry white wine
1 teaspoon curry powder
2 tablespoons minced shallots
1/2 cup heavy cream
Salt and pepper to taste

Garnish: fresh parsley

Preheat broiler.

Heat butter over medium-high heat in a medium skillet. Add escargot and sauté for 1 minute. Add the wine, curry powder and shallots and sauté until wine is reduced by half. Add the cream and bring to a slow boil and immediately remove from heat. Season with salt and pepper. Divide mixture among 4 small ramekins and broil until crispy on top. Serve immediately.

Châteaubriand with Peppercorn Sauce

TWO SERVINGS

Châteaubriand, which is actually a recipe and not a cut of meat, was named after the 19th century French author and statesman François Châteaubriand. The term, however, commonly refers to a thick steak cut from the center of a filet of beef.

2 pounds beef tenderloin
4 tablespoons butter
1/4 teaspoon black pepper
2 tablespoons green Madagascar peppercorns
1/2 cup veal stock
2 tablespoons Cognac
1/2 cup heavy cream

Prepare a medium-hot grill. Melt 2 tablespoons of the butter and coat the meat. Season with the black pepper. Place steak on grill and sear each side for 4 minutes. Remove meat from the grill.

Heat a large skillet over high heat. Add the meat, peppercorns and veal stock to the skillet and cook for 1 minute. Add the cognac and cook for another minute. Add the heavy cream and turn the steak. Cook until the sauce thickens enough to coat the back of a spoon. Remove the steak and serve with remaining peppercorn sauce.

Profiteroles with Chocolate Sauce

FOUR SERVINGS

For the Choux Paste:

1-1/4 cups whole milk
7 tablespoons butter
1/2 teaspoon salt
1 teaspoon sugar
1 cup flour
5 eggs

For the Chocolate Sauce:

10 ounces dark chocolate
3 tablespoons heavy cream

Vanilla ice cream

Preheat oven to 400°F.

Prepare the choux paste:
Place milk, butter, salt and sugar in a medium saucepan and slowly bring to a boil over medium-high heat. Simmer until the butter has melted completely. Remove the saucepan from the heat (but do not turn off the heat) and add all of the flour at once and mix thoroughly with a wooden spoon. Return the saucepan to the heat and continue mixing until the mixture forms a mass and the excess moisture has been eliminated, approximately 1 to 2 minutes. Remove from the heat and let the mixture cool slightly. Using a wooden spoon, beat in 1 egg at a time, making sure each egg is thoroughly incorporated and that the dough is smooth before adding the next egg.

Make the swan bodies:
Fit a pastry bag with a 3/4 inch tip and fill with two-thirds of the choux paste. Squeeze the dough onto a baking sheet, making 8 to 10 mounds 2 inches wide and 1 inch high. Bake for about 25 minutes. The puffs will have doubled in size and should be golden brown. Turn the oven off and remove the puffs. Pierce each puff with a skewer or a sharp knife and return the puffs to the oven, leaving the oven door ajar, for an additional 10 minutes.

Make the necks:
Fit a pastry bag with a 1/4-inch plain tip and squeeze out the remaining dough in "S" shaped swirls. Bake until the swirls are golden brown, about 5 to 8 minutes.

Prepare the chocolate sauce:
Melt the chocolate in the top of a double boiler. Whisk in the heavy cream.

To serve the profiteroles, slice each puff in half and fill each half with vanilla ice cream. Attach the swan's neck and spoon some of the chocolate sauce over the ice cream. Serve immediately.

WALL HOUSE

Leeks with Beet Coulis

Pan-Roasted Veal with Celeriac Fritter

Lamb in Puff Pastry

Chocolate Fondant Cake

GUSTAVIA
SAINT BARTHÉLEMY, F.W.I.
05 90 27 71 83

Of all of the leaps of faith which were made by people moving to St. Barths with the idea of opening a restaurant, the record for the longest surely belongs to Franck Mathevet and Denis Chevallier, who opened the Wall House restaurant in Gustavia on December 24, 2000.

Franck and Denis grew up in the mountains of France. They are winter people, not summer people. They prefer skiing in the French Alps to surfing in the Caribbean. Despite these facts, they have quickly acclimated themselves to St. Barths, overcome a host of obstacles and, in a few short years, propelled the Wall House to the forefront of the most popular restaurants on the island. The story of their remarkable odyssey says a lot about the requisites for a happy and successful life on St. Barths.

Both Franck and Denis were born into the restaurant business. Denis grew up on a farm on the Swiss border in the town of Marnaz where his parents operated a *pension* and restaurant. Franck was raised in Saulieu, outside of Dijon, where his grandfather owned a restaurant which was taken over and operated by his parents until they sold it a few years ago. Franck knew as a very young child that he wanted to be a chef and began his cooking career as an apprentice in 1983 at the age of thirteen. He was awarded the title of best apprentice in the Rhone-Alps region and then worked at Gavroche, a three-star Michelin restaurant in London, and the two-star L'Auberge du Pere Bise in Talloires, France where he held the position of Second Chef. Denis was in charge of the dining room at L'Auberge du Pere Bise, and the two became good friends.

In 1994, Franck and Denis heard about a restaurant called Le Bercail which was located in the little town of La Clusaz outside of Chamonix and going out of business. It occupied an eighteenth-century chalet near the very top of the ski area. They purchased the restaurant, and it quickly became very popular with skiers who would arrive bundled in blankets for dinner either by sled from a parking area several hundred meters above the restaurant or by Caterpillar tractor from the base of the mountain. The dining room featured a huge fireplace which doubled as an oven. To add to the warmth and intimacy of the experience, Franck and Denis gave each guest a pair of slippers to wear upon entering the restaurant. Despite the logistical challenges of getting people to and from the restaurant, Le Bercail averaged 10,000 meals each ski season.

Franck Mathevet and Denis Chevallier

Like many others who preceded them to St. Barths, however, Franck and Denis became frustrated with the heavy hand of French taxes and regulations and decided to sell Le Bercail at the height of its popularity in 1999. In searching for alternatives elsewhere, they first looked at a number of restaurants near ski areas just over the border in Switzerland but couldn't find anything in their price range. Just as they were beginning to regret selling Le Bercail, they heard about a failed restaurant by the name of The Wall House which was for sale in faraway St. Barths.

They traveled to the island for the first time in November of 2000. Their initial impressions of St. Barths were not encouraging. It seemed oppressively hot. They also learned that the Wall House had been closed for nearly two years. It thus had no goodwill upon which to build, and what reputation remained was, in fact, bad. There were no books to examine. Their inspection of the restaurant was limited to a single walk-through which revealed a dining room and kitchen in need of extensive renovations and repair. They had no intention of returning to France, however, and knew that they couldn't afford Switzerland. In a moment which they describe as one of "unconsciousness," they bought the business.

In hindsight, they say they would never have bought Wall House if they had known the challenges and obstacles which awaited them. After concluding the purchase, they returned to France where they faced the daunting task of assembling an entire staff for the restaurant and persuading them to pull up stakes and move several thousand miles to reopen a failed restaurant in the Caribbean. To make matters worse, they couldn't promise prospective employees anything specific by way of a salary because they had no idea whether or when the restaurant would make money. Instead, they offered recruits free lodging above the restaurant and urged them to "come and see" how much money they could all make. For most people, such a strategy would have been doomed to fail. Franck and Denis, however, were not only able to staff the restaurant in this fashion but have managed to retain most of their original Wall House employees.

The team arrived in Gustavia on December 14, 2000, and Franck and Denis were instantly confronted with a new set of problems. In the first place, they were informed that the local banks were no longer accepting commercial accounts leaving them no alternative but to deal with banks on St. Maarten. They also received a crash course on the challenges of obtaining food for a restaurant on a tiny island lacking the capacity to grow its own produce as they began calling suppliers only to learn that many of the ingredients they needed were unavailable and that those which the supplier had on hand cost over three times what they had cost in France. As the newcomers in the St. Barths' restaurant world, they were last in line for deliveries which often meant that even when they were assured that a particular ingredient was in stock when they placed an order in the morning, the supplier had run out of the requested item by the time he arrived at the Wall House. Needless to say, this necessitated a flexible approach by Franck in the kitchen and split-second menu changes.

The fact that the prior Wall House had been a failure was, of course, a major impediment to attracting customers. During the first few months of operation, there were many evenings when not a single person arrived for dinner. Realizing that it would take time to establish a good reputation for the Wall House, Franck and Denis decided to stay open seven days a week and twelve months a year for lunch and dinner. They even tried serving breakfast. They kept prices low (a practice which they continue to this day) so that they could win over the locals who had long since stopped patronizing the restaurant.

Some of the difficulties encountered by Franck and Denis were self-inflicted as well. They decided, for example, that they needed to build a fireplace so that they could cook over an open fire as they had done at Le Bercail only to discover that, because of the direction of the prevailing breezes in Gustavia, the smoke from the fire would often waft through the dining room leaving guests in tears and gasping for air. They were therefore forced to abandon the charcoal pit which can still be seen in all of its sooty glory in the rear of the restaurant. (In December of 2002 they made a second and successful foray into the world of

roasting meat, poultry and fish with the acquisition of a gleaming, modern and completely smokeless rotisserie).

Fortunately, their persistence has paid off, and the Wall House is packed each day for lunch and dinner. Their success is proof that with enough talent, hard work and determination, it is still possible to start from scratch and create lives of distinction on St. Barths. It is clear, however, that a good sense of humor has played a key role in their success as well. Franck and Denis are two of the most likeable people on St. Barths, and they have kept everything – the good and the bad – in perspective. The bigger the catastrophe, the funnier and more entertaining the memory. They recount their early travails with banks and suppliers with an air of bemused wonderment that they somehow managed to get through it all. They laugh so hard describing the charcoal pit saga that tears rivaled only by those caused by the smoky fire itself roll down their cheeks. Disasters are no match for the sunny and sanguine dispositions of these good-natured friends. Their cups are always at least half full, and life has been and will likely continue to be very good indeed.

Leeks with Beet Coulis

FOUR SERVINGS

The menu at the Wall House refers to this dish as a "Leek Salad in a Red Dress". This colorful appetizer is at its best when it is served very cold.

4 large leeks

For the Beet Coulis:

2 beets

5 tablespoons red wine vinegar

1/2 cup soy oil

Salt and pepper to taste

Prepare the beet coulis:
Preheat oven to 450°F. Trim the beets, leaving approximately 1 inch of stem attached to each. Wrap beets in aluminum foil and roast in the middle of the oven for one hour.

When beets are cool enough to handle, slip off skin and slice into several pieces. Puree the beets in a food processor or blender with the soy oil and vinegar. Add salt and pepper to taste. Chill the sauce.

Prepare the leeks:
Trim the leeks and discard the tough outer leaves. Split the leeks lengthwise and thoroughly rinse under cold running water.

Bring a large saucepan of salted water to a boil. Reduce heat to medium-low and add the leeks. Simmer until the leeks are tender but can still hold their shape, approximately 20 to 25 minutes. Drain the leeks and refresh with cold water. Slice leeks into 1/2 inch slices and chill.

Spoon some of the beet sauce on a plate and arrange the poached leeks in a triangle on top of the beet sauce.

Pan Roasted Veal with Celeriac Fritter

FOUR SERVINGS

1 veal tenderloin, trimmed and cut crosswise into 4 tournedos (ask your butcher for the trimmings for the sauce)
2 tablespoons butter

For the Sauce:
1 carrot, chopped
1 shallot, chopped
4 cups veal stock
1 small bunch parsley, tied
5 sun-dried tomatoes
2 tablespoons unsalted butter

For the Celeriac Fritter
2 pounds potatoes, peeled
1/2 celeriac, peeled
1 egg
2 tablespoons peanut oil
2 teaspoons butter

For the Celeriac Garnish:
1/2 cup julienned celeriac
Vegetable oil for deep frying

Garnish: chopped parsley and minced sun-dried tomato

Prepare the sauce:
In a large saucepan, cook veal trimmings, carrots and shallots over medium heat until the vegetables soften. Add the veal stock and parsley bundle and simmer over medium-low heat for 15 minutes. Remove the parsley bundle and puree the parsley along with 3 sun-dried tomatoes in a blender. Return the parsley puree to the stock pan and reduce over medium heat until the sauce thickens enough to coat the back of a spoon. Pass the sauce through a sieve and season it with salt and pepper. Reduce the heat to low and whisk in 2 tablespoons of butter.

Prepare the fritters:
Reserve 3 very fine slices of celeriac. Grate the potatoes and celeriac in a bowl. Season with salt and pepper and mix in the egg. Heat 2 tablespoons of the peanut oil in a medium skillet over medium-high heat. Working in batches, drop the celeriac/potato mixture by 1/3 cupfuls, pressing down on each to create a 3-inch round. Cook for 5 minutes. Add 2 teaspoons of butter to the pan and cook for an additional 5 minutes. Carefully flip the fritters and cook for 10 more minutes. Transfer to a baking sheet and keep warm in the oven.

Prepare the veal and celeriac garnish:
Pan sear the veal tournedos with butter, about 8 minutes per side over medium -high heat. While the veal is cooking, heat 1 inch of oil to 375°F and fry the julienned celeriac until golden, approximately 10 to 15 seconds. Serve the veal on a fritter with the sauce. Garnish with the celeriac julienne, chopped parsley and minced sun-dried tomato.

Lamb in Puff Pastry

FOUR SERVINGS

For the Lamb:

4 loin lamb chops, each about 1 inch thick, trimmed
2 tablespoons peanut oil
4 6-inch squares puff pastry, thawed
1 egg, beaten

For the Marinade:

1 carrot, chopped
1 onion, diced
2 garlic cloves, minced
1/2 cup gin
1 bottle red wine
1 celery stick, chopped
2 tablespoons juniper berries
1 tablespoon paprika
1 teaspoon fresh thyme leaves

For the Grand Veneur Sauce:

1 cup brown chicken stock
1 cup heavy cream
2 tablespoons cranberry jam
Salt and pepper to taste
2 tablespoons peanut oil

For the Breadcrumbs:

1 cup of fresh breadcrumbs
1 tablespoon freshly chopped parsley
1 clove garlic, minced

The lamb is prepared in a style usually reserved for venison and is paired with a grand veneur sauce, which is a classic sauce often served with game. The lamb goes beautifully with braised red cabbage or potato gratin.

Combine the marinade ingredients. Marinade the lamb in the refrigerator for at least 8 hours and up to 3 days.

Remove the lamb from the marinade, reserving the marinade, and pat the lamb dry.

Boil the reserved marinade over medium-high heat until it is reduced by half. Add the chicken stock and reduce by half again. Add the heavy cream and cranberry jam and cook for 10 more minutes until sauce is a bit thicker. Pass through a sieve and season with salt, pepper, paprika and juniper berries to taste.

While the sauce is reducing, toast the breadcrumbs on a cookie sheet for 5 minutes at 300°F. Combine the breadcrumbs with the chopped parsley and minced garlic. Coat the lamb with the breadcrumbs. Heat the peanut oil in a large skillet over very high heat. Very briefly (2-3 seconds) pan sear each side of the lamb.

Let the lamb cool and then wrap each piece in one of the puff pastry squares, sealing the edge with a bit of water. Brush the top of the pastry with the beaten egg. Place the lamb on parchment paper and freeze for 2 hours.

Preheat oven to 425°F.

Reheat the sauce over medium-low heat. Roast the lamb until the puff pastry turns golden, approximately 15 minutes. Slice the lamb and present on a plate with the sauce. Garnish with fresh cranberries and chestnuts.

Chocolate Fondant Cake

SIX SERVINGS

These warm chocolate cakes should be slightly underbaked and are especially delicious if made with a specialty baking chocolate such as Lindt or Valrhona.

1 stick unsalted butter
5 ounces bittersweet (not unsweetened) chocolate, chopped
4 medium size eggs
1/2 cup superfine sugar
1/2 cup flour

Garnish: coconut or vanilla ice cream

Melt butter and chocolate in a medium saucepan over low heat until smooth.

Using an electric mixer, beat eggs and gradually add in the sugar. Add the flour at once and beat until thoroughly combined. Fold in half of the chocolate mixture and stir to combine. Fold in remaining chocolate mixture. Let the batter rest for 1 hour in the refrigerator.

Generously butter small individual non-stick tart molds.

Preheat oven to 425°F. Fill the tart molds with the batter and bake for 6 to 8 minutes. Gently turn the cakes out of the molds on a plate and serve immediately with the coconut or vanilla ice cream.

RESOURCES

Asian ingredients:

Uwajimaya
519 6th Avenue South
Seattle, WA 98104
1-800-889-1928
www.uwajimaya.com

My Spicer
1510 W. Fairmont, Suite C
Longview, TX 75604
1-903-553-0800
www.myspicer.com

Cheese starters, fresh fromage blanc and mascarpone:

New England Cheese Making
Supply Company
Ashfield, MA 01330
(413) 628-3808
www.cheesemaking.com

Duck, foie gras, squab and rendered duck fat:

D'Artagan
280 Wilson Avenue
Newark, NJ 07105
1-800-327-8246
www.dartagnan.com

Hudson Valley Foie Gras
80 Brooks Road
Ferndale, NY 12734
1-845-292-2500
www.hudsonvalleyfoiegras.com

Fresh fish and shellfish:

Browne Trading Company
Merrill's Wharf
Portland, Maine
1-800-944-7848
www.browne-trading.com

Frog's legs:

Cajun Grocer
208 W. Pinhook Rd.
Lafayette, LA 70503
1-888-272-9347
www.cajungrocer.com

Salmon (Copper River) - available mid-May to mid-June:

Browne Trading Company
Merrill's Wharf
Portland, Maine
1-800-944-7848
www.browne-trading.com

Prime Select Seafoods
P.O. Pox 846
Cordova, Alaska 99574
1-888-870-7292
www.pssifish.com

Salt cod, dried:

Dean & Deluca
560 Broadway
New York, NY 10012
1-800-221-7714
www.dean-deluca.com

Truffles:

Urbani Truffles
29-24 40th Avenue
Long Island City, NY 11104
1-800-281-2330
www.urbani.com

Marché aux Delices
120 Imlay Street
Brooklyn, NY 11231
1-888-547-5471
www.auxdelices.com